MARY ROSE'S

1001 COUNTRY DIY HINTS

MARY ROSE'S

*1001 COUNTRY
DIY HINTS*

Published in the UK exclusively for

SELECTABOOK
Folly Road
Roundway
Devizes
Wiltshire
SN10 2HT

Produced by TAJ BOOKS
27 Ferndown Gardens
Cobham
Surrey
KT11 2BH

Email: info@tajbooks.com

ISBN 1-84406-17-9

Printed and bound in China

CONTENTS

* * * * *

DABBLING AT DECORATING

9

THE PLUMBER'S MATE

33

AN ELECTRIC CURRENT

45

INVALUABLE TOOL KIT

51

FIXING & BONDING

57

SAFETY AT WORK

79

FIXTURES & FITTINGS

85

THE BUILDERS YARD

93

CAR MAINTENANCE

107

GLOSSARY OF D.I.Y TERMS

119

INDEX

124

ACKNOWLEDGEMENTS

I would like to dedicate this book to my father Frank as he is quite handy at the DIY. My thanks to Joe for his help with the book and for putting the hints into practice around the house. To Karen, Arleen, Orla, Cathal and Brenda, I am grateful for their support and encouragement.

INTRODUCTION

*"Ability is what you're capable of doing.
Motivation determines what you do.
Attitude determines how well you do it."*

Many people look on DIY as a hobby but in reality for most people it is part of our daily lives. Whether it is fixing a leaky tap or wiring a plug it is useful to know how to do it yourself rather than always having to call a plumber or electrician.

This collection of valuable hints and tips includes information on decorating, plumbing, electrical work, carpentry, building and car maintenance. Some hints are informative while others are constantly useful and should make DIY tasks more easily completed. Natural products are used when appropriate.

Safety in the workshop and on the job must always take first priority and no risks should be taken. Always call on professional help if in doubt about your ability to do any work especially electrical.

The chapter on tools gives a factual look at what implements would be helpful to have around the house or to give to someone starting up a new home. The poems and proverbs included always give me great delight and I hope they make the book more enjoyable.

I have had great pleasure in compiling this practical book from hints and tips that I have acquired over the years. I hope that there is something of interest for you in it and that you find it helpful, interesting and entertaining. Most of all let it be useful to you whether DIY is a hobby or a regular chore.

MARY ROSE

*"If at first you don't succeed,
Remove all evidence you ever tried."*

DABBLING AT DECORATING

Make up your mind to be happy.
Learn to find pleasure in simple things.
Make the best of circumstance.
No one has everything, and everyone has something of sorrow.
Don't take yourself too seriously.
Don't let criticism worry you - you can't please everyone.
Don't let your neighbours set your standards - be yourself.
Do things you enjoy doing, but stay out of debt.
Don't borrow trouble.
Imaginary things are harder to bear than actual ones.
Since hate poisons the soul, do not cherish grudges.
Avoid people who make you unhappy.
Have many interests. If you can't travel read about places.
Don't hold post-mortems or spend time brooding over sorrows and mistakes.
Don't be the one who never gets over things.
Keep busy at something.
A very busy person never has time to be unhappy.
Robert Louis Stevenson

PLANNING

Before commencing decorating it is useful to compile a decorating file to help co-ordinate a project. This can hold magazine pictures, photos, paint colour cards, samples of material or wallpaper and any sketches with measurements. This information will be useful to take on shopping trips.

Make a measured floor plan of the room to be decorated. Use graph paper and sketch the room, recording the room dimensions, window and door sizes and placement, and the location of radiators, electrical outlets and any other permanent fixtures.

Acquire a light 10'(3m) tape for carrying around while a 25'(10m) tape is more useful for measuring at home.

Add several pens or pencils and a large pad of paper or spiral notebook for taking notes, sketching furniture possibilities, and marking pages of sample books.

A diary can be very helpful to keep track of dates for carpet installation, when your wallpaper order will be in, or what day the painter will phone with an estimate.

Keep a list of phone numbers for a project, including the paint store, the carpet salesman, the upholsterer, etc.

A small roll of tape and a small pair of scissors can be useful to snip fabric o r carpet samples.

Always have a sample of anything staying in the room, including carpeting, upholstery fabric, paint samples, tile, wood, etc. With upholstery, take an arm cover or a cushion cover or a good colour photo of the item and try to snip a small piece of fabric from inside a seam or underneath in an inconspicuous area, tape these to the back of the photo.

Take a small piece of leftover carpeting or snip some carpet fibres from several hidden areas of a room (behind doors, in corners, under a metal door strip) until there is enough to see the colour. Then tape or staple them to a piece of white cardboard and keep it safely in an envelope.

Bring a few plain envelopes in your bag. They are useful to keep samples from shops separate and easily identified when any relevant information is written on the envelope.

Post it notes can be placed on magazine photos to make notes or used to mark pages under consideration in wallpaper books.

"Speed and accuracy do not agree "

PAINTING PREPARATION

When painting a room with good surfaces the preparation and clean up will take half as much time as the actual painting. If the surfaces are in poor condition then the non-painting time could take longer than the painting.

The best conditions for decorating are working in daylight in a well-ventilated room. Turn off the heating as circulating air is the best for drying. Heat can cause uneven patches if an area dries out too quickly.

Generally ceilings should be painted first, then walls and woodwork. The only exception to this is, if the ceiling is to be painted a darker colour than the walls then the lighter colour should be applied first and it will not be as noticeable if it strays on to the ceiling as the darker colour will cover it. Make sure the light paint is completely dry before painting the darker colour.

Before painting or papering a room make sure the surface is well prepared and smooth. Defects in wall plaster will be more noticeable when the wall has a fresh coat of paint.

Counter sink any visible nails and dab the nail heads with oil paint and allow too dry before applying emulsion paint.

Wash walls with detergent to remove any grease or dirt. Rinse thoroughly and give adequate time to dry before painting.

Sugar soap is excellent for washing down walls before painting. It comes in powder or concentrated liquid form. Dissolve well in warm water before applying to the wall with a sponge or brush. Work in well to any badly stained areas. Leave on the walls for a few minutes before rinsing off thoroughly. Allow the wall to dry before painting.Sugar soap can be an irritant. Wear rubber gloves and avoid contact with the eyes.

Fill all holes, cracks, seams and imperfections with filler or caulk. Sand any rough surfaces with fine sandpaper.

When using cellulose filler, remove any loose material from the crack or hole. Push the filler in with a putty knife, leaving the surface slightly proud as plaster and filler will shrink as they dry. Sand flat when dry.

"Never put off till tomorrow what you can do today"

PAINTING PREPARATION

Fill all hairline cracks as they will eventually show through paint-work or paper.

When filling deep large holes or cracks in plaster, fill in two stages, half at the time, letting the first half dry before inserting the second.

If the edging of the plaster around a window is damaged, use corner beading to form a new edge.

Most fillers and plaster are white. When using dark coloured paint the filler should be mixed with the paint being used rather than water so that the repair is not visible. Note that drying agents are used in paint so the filler may set more quickly when mixed with paint.

The easiest way to cover furniture in a room to be decorated is to move it all to the middle of the room and cover with old throws or sheets.

Light fixtures that are difficult to take down, can be covered by taping large plastic bags around them.

Slip old socks over your shoes to avoid paint spots.

Do not use plastic sheeting on the floor as it can be very slippery and particularly dangerous when working on steps.

As well as paint and thinners, brushes, rollers and trays, some of the other tools and material, you will require are listed below: -

Step ladders, to help you reach elevated areas
Drop cloths - to protect furniture, floors etc from paint.Paint scrapers, flat and triangular - to remove loose or peeling paint from wood, plaster, and other surfaces
Steel wool - to remove corrosion from metal surfaces
Scrubbing brush - to remove mildew and dirt
Bristle brush and Wire brush - to clear loose material from masonry
Putty knife - to scrape away loose paint, or to apply filler
Sandpaper (various grades) and a sanding block - to smooth previously painted surfaces, or to roughen glossy surfaces so paint will adhere better
Tubes of caulk and caulking gun - to apply caulk to cracks in walls or woodwork.
Masking tape - to protect windowpanes and trim from paint
Paint guide - to protect carpets and walls when painting baseboards and other trim
A selection of rags - to mop up spills or rub paint off hands.

"Success is very often failure with a new coat of paint"

SANDING

Sandpaper or glass paper is sandy looking paper and comes in grades from extremely coarse to very fine.

Black coloured paper for sanding is called 'wet and dry'. It is coated with silicone carbine. It can be used dry or slightly dampened. This paper is generally used for sanding paint or metal. When using wet it leaves a sludgy mess that needs to be constantly wiped off. It should only be kept damp, not soaked in water.

Emery paper is also black but is very tough and only used on metal especially for removing rust. Lubricate with paraffin to prevent clogging.

Emery cloth is only used on metals. The backing gives it extra strength so it is useful for curved work. Lubricate with paraffin. For even sanding, use each successive grade at right angles to the direction of the previous one.

Wire or steel wool is made from lengths of fine steel strips rolled together. It is useful for removing rust, paint or ground in dirt. For tougher jobs use a wire brush.

When sanding with any paper, start with a coarse grade and work down gradually to finer grades until the required smoothness of the finish is achieved.

Most sheets of sandpaper will only have the grade mark in one corner, to know which grade used when a section is torn off mark the grade on it.

To strengthen sandpaper, tape wide strips of masking tape across the back.

When sanding flat surfaces, wrap the paper around a cork or rubber sanding-block, this will keep the paper flat and in contact with the surface for even sanding. It also prevents fingers from becoming irritated.

To sand inside a narrow slit, wrap sandpaper round the blunt side of a hacksaw blade to make it easy to handle.

To unclog sandpaper put the back of it against the edge of a piece of wood or table and drag the paper to and fro across it to open the grain.

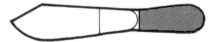

"It's better to have it and not need it than to need it and not have it!"

SANDING

Do not use old abrasive paper. The irregular surface of the worn surface can cause scratching. Always use new paper.

Bare wood and plaster should be dry-sanded. This will produce a lot of dust so wear a suitable protective mask.Sand old paint-work with 'wet and dry' sandpaper.

On wood, always sand with the grain rather than across it.

Painted surfaces are more quickly rubbed down using a wet technique as the water acts as a lubricant Wrap the appropriate sandpaper around a rubber block, dip in a bucket of water and sand in the normal way. While working, regularly rinse the paper, rub on a piece of soap to lubricate it and always keep it wet. The surface should be rinsed afterwards using clean water and a sponge. Allow to dry before repainting.

There are three types of power sanders:-
The belt sander is a heavy-duty machine that has a continuous belt of abrasive paper rotating on two rollers. The grade of paper is easily changed. Dust from the machine is collected in an attached dust bag.

The orbital sander is a finishing tool. The base of the tool is fitted with felt or rubber padding and the sanding sheets are secured to the sole plate by clamps at each end. Two hands should be used when working the tool and the proper grade of sandpaper for the job in hand.

The disc sander comes as a drill attachment. Sanding discs of different grades are available. The machine can be difficult to control if the whole face of the disc is used so tilt the wheel slightly and use light pressure.

With all power-sanders :-
Always switch off the power on the machine and at the supply before changing sanding sheets or discs.
Never leave the machine standing on work.
Lift the machines by their handles.
Avoid unnecessary re-sanding.
Use care at corners so that they are not mistakenly rounded.
Work with the grain, especially when doing finishing work.
Pressure should be applied light and evenly or ridges will form.
Do not allow the sanding sheet to become clogged.
Regularly clean the machines to keep them free of dust.

To fine-finish decorative wood surfaces prior to varnishing, use fine steel wool. Always work with the grain of the wood to avoid scratches across the grain.

"Time is a file that wears and makes no noise. "

STRIPPING PAINT

Before painting over old semi-gloss paint, check that it has not become brittle. Try picking off a piece from an obscure area. If it chips then give the whole paint-work a light sanding to improve the texture for the new paint.

When using chemicals to strip paint -
Adequately protect the floor under the work area.
Wear eye goggles and strong gloves.
Use disposable brushes and discard when finished.
Apply a generous covering of solvent.
Leave on for the required time.
Scrape off with a putty knife then rub with fine steel wool.
Work in a well-ventilated area.

Caustic soda (sodium hydroxide) can be used to strip items that can be taken outdoors. Half fill a large, strong, plastic bucket with hot water and standing well back add 4-8ozs(100 - 225g) caustic soda, stir with a long stick. **(NEVER add water to the soda as the first dash of water will cause the soda to erupt and spew upwards, giving off very strong fumes).**

The temperature of the water and the amount of soda required is determined by the toughness of the paint to be removed. Varnish will come off more easily than paint. The hotter the water the more effective the result **but beware of the fumes.**

Brush on the liquid with a plastic washing-up brush. Leave on until the paint is bubbling and very soft. Hose off with a power hose or with a brush and bucket of water. The process may need to be repeated if there is more than one layer of paint. Obstinate patches can be treated, by mixing the solution with flour or cornflour to hold it in place. Paint on the area and leave for an hour.

Caustic soda should never be in contact with tin or galvanised iron. Do not apply soda with a paint-brush as the bristles will fall out from the metal holding them.

When using caustic soda, always wear thick, hole free, rubber gloves, wellingtons, goggles and perhaps a plastic coat. **If caustic soda splashes on the skin it will burn it.** As it burns slowly you may not immediately feel the pain until there is a hole is the skin. Any skin splashed should be rinsed with plenty of cold water immediately.

"The trouble with experience is that by the time you have it, you are too old to take advantage of it"

STRIPPING PAINT

When all the paint is stripped off, wipe down with equal parts of vinegar and water to neutralise the caustic in the grain.

Hose down the working area with plenty of water. Keep animals and children away from the area when working with caustic soda. Never leave the area unattended.

Caustic soda may cause colour changes in wood and a very strong solution can cause small black spots.

To avoid mess when stripping paint and varnish, take an empty paint can and cut a slot in the side ensuring that it is wider and deeper than the paint scraper. Run the scraper through the slot to remove the stripped waste.

Another method of stripping paint is with a blowtorch. Never apply this to metal or plaster walls.

Play the hot flame of the torch on the painted timber and it will make the paint bubble up. Remove the paint with a scraper.

Do not keep the flame on one area for too long or it can burn the wood. Remove a light burn by sanding the area.

Great care must be taken if using a blowtorch to strip window-frames as the flame can crack the glass. A sheet of metal can be used as a shield. Remember that the metal can become hot and burn the hands so wear cotton gloves.

Use protective sheeting beneath the work area as hot paint lumps call fall off and damage the surface below. Keep a bucket of water nearby in case of an accidental fire.

Use an electric hot air gun to strip paint off awkward areas.

Broad, flat scrapers are used for large areas while triangular ones are best for awkward corners.

When the paint is removed, sand the surface with first a medium and then a fine grade sandpaper.

On tough metals in guttering or drain-pipes do not use a blowtorch to remove the paint. Use a wire brush. Efficient wire brush attachments can be purchased for electric drills. Chemical paint strippers can also be used.

Paint cellulose wallpaper paste over old emulsion to help remove it. Leave on for 10 minutes before scraping.

"It destroys the craft not to learn it "

CHOOSING PAINT

Knotting should be applied to bare woodwork. Cover any visible knots to prevent any resinous substance from leaking out. It is important to apply knotting to outdoor woodwork as the heat from the sun can cause the resin to swell and seep through the paint-work.

Primer paint is applied to a surface to give a base for subsequent coats of paint. All-purpose primer can be used for any surface. However specific primers are available for different surfaces.

Acrylic primer/undercoat is water based and can be applied to interior or exterior surfaces, cement, woodwork, hardboard, brickwork and new or old plaster. Never use on bare metal unless it has been first primed with a metal primer and allowed to dry. Undercoat is useful if changing the colour of the surface from dark to light and it can reduce the amount of topcoat paint required

Alkali-resisting primer is oil based and is used to bind powdery surfaces such as plaster or brick.

Aluminium wood-primer is oil based and is used to seal resinous timber or on surfaces previously treated with coal-tar preservatives.

Calcium plumbate primer is an all-purpose primer. It can be used as a first coat on galvanised or on wood and metal window frames. It is an excellent rust inhibitor.

Lead-based wood primer is restricted to outside use as it is toxic, while lead-free wood primer can be used on interior wood surfaces.

Zinc phosphate metal primer was developed as an alternative to red lead. It can be used for all ferrous metal surfaces and is and excellent rust inhibitor.

Zinc chromate metal-primer is a universal metal primer suitable for interior or exterior work and is a rust inhibitor.

Oil or resin undercoat is used under gloss paint to enhance the finished work.

Gloss paint is oil based and is very tough and durable. It is mainly used on interior and exterior woodwork. It can be used on kitchen or bathroom walls but tends to encourage condensation and can be difficult to apply to a large area.

"Work expands so as to fill the time available"

CHOOSING PAINT

Polyurethane paints also have a tough hard-wearing finish and they do not require an undercoat. They are generally used on radiators, pipes and metal surfaces.

Eggshell paint is oil based but not as tough as gloss and is generally only used for interior work. Use on metal, woodwork or walls as it does not encourage condensation. Make sure the room is well ventilated when working as these paints have a strong smell and are slow drying. Apply an undercoat if painting wood as the surface is absorbent.

Emulsion paints are water based and are quick drying. They are essentially wall paint and are unsuitable for woodwork or metal. Matt emulsion should be used instead of silk finish where there tends to be condensation. Anti-condensation emulsion is available and it may contain a fungicide that deters mould growth.

Thixotropic paints are non-drip and can be either gloss or flat. They have a solid jelly like texture. When a brush or roller is pressed into the paint it temporarily becomes liquid and loads on to it. The paint then solidifies again until it is spread onto a surface. Do not stir this paint even if it looks lumpy or it will become liquid and no longer be non-drip. Non-drip emulsions are useful for painting ceilings while non-drip gloss is good for woodwork.

Textured paints are good to hide small cracks and imperfections in walls and ceilings. They are thick and leave a rough finish. When the paint is applied with a roller it will leave a stippled finish. Some of these textured paints have to be painted over with emulsion when they are dry.

Stone paints give a strong protection to external walls. Always follow the manufacturer's instructions.

Specialist paints are used for specific work, these include paint for tiles, linoleum, bath enamels and heat resistant paints.

Thin oil-based paints with white spirits and water-based paints with water.

DIY and hardware shops can mix paint to an exact colour and have a wide range of colour cards. Make sure to keep a note of the exact colour mixed should you later require more.

"The old believe everything,
The middle aged suspect everything,
The young know everything"

Try to get a few paint samples before choosing a colour. Apply the samples on the two sides of a corner so that colour changes due to reflections from the light of two different angles can be seen.

The amount of paint required will depend on, paint type, number of coats required and the condition of the surface to be painted.

Stir paint thoroughly before each use and periodically while painting.

To salvage lumpy paint cut a circle from a piece of wire screen slightly smaller than the circumference of the tin. Push the wire circle down the tin and the lumps will go to the bottom. Another way is to strain the paint through an old sieve or old nylon stockings.

To easily find a tin of paint for reuse, always store the paint in its original container, with the label intact. If the label is covered with paint drippings, write down the brand, manufacturer's code, colour, gloss level and type of paint on a strip of masking tape and stick it to the side of the can before storing. Other useful information such as the room the paint was used for can also be added.

To mark the level of paint in a can, put a rubber band around the can and roll it down to the level of the paint inside. Or dip a stick into the can and this will give the exact depth of the paint in the tin. When it dries attach it to the outside of the tin with a strong rubber band.

Store small amounts of paint in jam jars. Screw the lid on tightly and store upside down.

Most paint will differ slightly in each lot produced so purchase enough to complete the job.

"Experience is a wonderful thing
It enables you to recognise a mistake
When you make it again "

CHOOSING PAINT

Always seal the paint container tightly between paint jobs to prevent it from thickening or evaporating. To seal a can properly, clean excess paint from the rim with a brush and then gently tap the edge of the cover with a hammer.

To prevent air from entering partially used paint cans, place the lid firmly on and store them upside down.

To save time when painting stand the paint tin in warm water for 30 minutes. This will make the paint easier to apply, reduce drips and provide better coverage.

Never store paint in extreme cold (below zero) or extremely hot conditions (over 100°F/38°C). Although most paints are formulated to withstand several freeze-thaw cycles, these conditions cause them to solidify.

A piece of string tied across the top of a paint tin can support the wet brush and it can also be used to wipe off excess paint.

Take time to read the instructions on the paint tin. Note the type of thinner to be used and the amount required.

Generally paint should only be thinned slightly to make it more manageable.

If a large tin of paint has been purchased, decant the amount required for the job in hand, into a paint kettle or another container with a handle, before thinning.

To avoid getting paint on the rim of a paint tin when pouring, put a strip of masking tape over half the rim. Pour out the paint over the tape area. When finished remove the tape and the lid can be resealed cleanly.

A simple drip-catching tray can be made by cutting a circle, the diameter of the paint tin, out of the side of a empty cereal or detergent packet. Set the tin in the box and this will catch any drips. Or sit the tin on a large paper plate.

Bend a pipe cleaner into a triangle at one end and use for touching up small paint jobs.

Remove paint or dye colouring stains from skin by washing with shaving cream and water.

Use cooking oil and sugar to help remove oil-based paint from hands.

"Nothing is so fatiguing as the eternal hanging on
of uncompleted tasks."

Brushes & Rollers

It is worth buying expensive paintbrushes and with good care they can be reused many times without the bristles becoming loose. Choose brushes with split ends to the bristles as this is a sign of good quality.

The bristles on pure bristle brushes come from wild pigs or boars found in China and India. Chinese bristles are black in colour, of high quality and very resilient. Indian bristles vary in colour, are coarse, longer in length and less resilient.

Some brushes are composed of a mixture of horsehair and bristle to produce a softer, cheaper brush.

Since pure bristle is very expensive most brushes are made from synthetic fibre. They are hard wearing and resistant to many chemicals.

Very cheap brushes should only be used if they are being discarded after one use. Avoid brushes with short bristles as their paint holding capacity is low.

Most brushes will shed a few bristles and cheap brushes shed many of theirs in the first few strokes. Loose bristles can be dislodged if the brush is worked back and forth in the palm of the hand for a few minutes. Paint the first few strokes of paint in an inconspicuous area.

Before dipping the brush in the paint, pre-dampen it slightly so that the paint is applied more evenly. When working with latex paints, moisten brushes with water, with oil-based paints, dip them in paint thinner then use paper towels to remove excess thinner.

When a brush has been used with colour paint, no matter how well it is cleaned, residue pigment can discolour white paint, so it is advisable to keep a couple of brushes for white paint only.

A block brush is used to apply cement paint. Its tough bristles are not damaged when working on a rough surface.

A crevice brush has a long metal handle that can be bent to any angle. It is useful for painting behind radiators or pipes.

*"The world is full of willing people:
some willing to work and some willing to let them"*

BRUSHES & ROLLERS

A cutting-in brush has the ends of the bristles trimmed at an angle to give better control when painting a straight line or painting around doors or windows.

Rollers are useful for painting large areas but corners or around fittings will have to be covered with a brush. Extension handles can be attached to rollers for painting high walls or ceilings.

Use a sheepskin roller if possible as they hold more paint than nylon pile rollers. However they are not suitable for applying gloss paint as they leave a slightly textured finish.

Avoid foam or sponge rollers as they absorb too much paint and leave bubbles in the paint surface.

Soak a new roller in warm soapy water for a few hours to remove loose fibres. Rinse and dry thoroughly before use.

To save time in cleaning up - before adding paint to the tray either line it with aluminium foil, or put the tray in a loose plastic bag. This will shape into the tray when the paint is added. Tie the end of the bag when the paint is on it. When finished painting, discard the bag.

Foam pads are light, splash free and light to use. However the finish can be disappointing. Like rollers they are useful in large areas but not corners.

When stopping painting for a short time or until the following day, wrap brushes or rollers in cling-film or aluminium foil and leave them in a cool place.

Always use the correct solvent to clean up paint equipment. Check the paint can label.

Use hot water and soap for water-based paints. First wipe off as much excess as possible. Hold the brush under hot running water, soap the bristles and squeeze out the paint. When clean rinse thoroughly. Shake well and leave to dry.

Do not leave paint-brushes standing in water as this can swell the wood and make the bristles loose.

Mineral spirits are used to clean brushes used with oil paint, enamel, and varnish. Acetone used for epoxies, alcohol for shellac. Observe all fire, ventilation, and safety precautions.

"Be master of your petty annoyances
And conserve your energies for the big, worthwhile things.
It isn't the mountain ahead that wears you out -
It's the grain of sand in your shoe."

An effective cleaner for oil-based paint-brushes is paraffin and it can be reused. Leave the jar overnight and the paint will fall to the bottom. The clear paraffin can be poured into another jar and used again.

After cleaning brushes with paraffin, wash them in warm soapy water and dry with a clean rag

To clean oil-based paint from brushes or rollers, wear plastic gloves and work the solvent into bristles or nap, then wash in warm soapy water, rinse well. To ensure that the brush keeps its shape, place an elastic band around the bristles.

A simple way to clean a brush with spirit is to put a little spirit into a strong plastic bag. Put the brush it the bag and work the spirit into the bristles with your fingers through the plastic.

Change paintbrushes every few hours - if the same paintbrush is used all day the paint will harden in it and make it very difficult to clean.

To soften hard paintbrushes boil up some vinegar, then soak the brushes in it. They will be restored to soft, usable brushes again.

Smooth clean bristles with an old comb. Once completely dry, store brushes hanging bristles down in their original wrap or paper. Rollers should be allowed to dry and stored standing on end.

When cleaning oil-based tools with paint thinner or mineral spirit, pour the liquid into a clean bucket and rinse the tools thoroughly. When done allow the solids to settle to the bottom of the bucket. Carefully strain the liquid back into its original container for reuse.

Conserve paint thinner when cleaning brushes by using a tall narrow container instead of a short flat one. This will minimise the amount of thinner required to reach all the bristles.

"The eye should be blind in the home of another"

DOORS & STAIRS

When painting a door, a sheet of cardboard under the door will prevent the brush picking up dust. Use two wedges to keep the door in position so that both sides can be painted.

Before painting doors remove all metal such as door handles or cover with masking tape. If paint does splash on the metal wipe off immediately with a soft cloth.

Oil paint is the most difficult to apply. When painting a flush door, start at the top corner on the hinge side. Load a 3"(7.5cm) brush and make three vertical stripes a brush width apart and 10"(25cm) long. With an empty brush stroke at right angles to these spreading the paint totally across the area. Finally with a dry brush, lightly stroke vertically over the area. Overlapping the first strokes into the painted areas, paint the remainder of the door in the same way, ending at the bottom corner on the handle side.

When painting panels and framework in different colours paint one colour first and leave to dry for three days. Mask with tape before applying the second colour to prevent the colours bleeding into each other.

Panelled doors should be painted top to bottom. On each panel, first paint the moulding then the interior. Finish with the outer edge. Work slightly outwards at the edges rather than inwards to avoid 'fat edges'.

To determine what part of the frame belongs to which room when painting - all frame edges up to and including the ones against which the door closes belong to the room into which it opens.

Paint the frame before the door. Painting it afterwards can lead to the brush marking the semi-dry paint on the door.

Always seal the top and bottom edges of doors with a finish coat to prevent moisture being absorbed and for easier cleaning.

If two coats of paint are required, make sure the first coat is completely dry before applying the second. Although some paints may feel dry to touch, for best results it is important to adhere to the specified drying times.

When painting stairs, start with the underside of each step overhang, then paint the risers and the treads. If stairs need to be used regularly then only paint alternate treads one day and the remainder the next so that they are still accessible.

"Nothing in this world can take the place of persistence."

PAINTING LARGE AREAS

Regularly masking tape is used to protect areas adjacent to the area to be painted. Make sure the paint is very dry before covering with masking tape.

Avoid covering the masking tape with too much paint. Remove it just as the paint begins to dry. If the tape is removed when the paint is still wet it can still run. If the paint has totally dried, the edge of the painted area can come off with the tape.

Pull the tape off very slowly and carefully. Lift the top edge of the tape and pull it back on itself, keeping it parallel with the wall, pull slowly and evenly.

Instead of using masking tape on a curved or rounded surface, paint on rubber cement. Any paint drips on the cement will come away when the cement is rubbed of.

Start painting near a window and work with the light in front. Finish each area in the same direction.

If using a roller, paint the corners of the room and where the ceiling and roof meets with a brush as the roller will not cover these areas.

Using a spray gun rather than a roller or brush gives the option of varying colour schemes by fading and layering colours. To achieve this, keep moving closer or farther away from the surface. To ensure a smooth finish, move at a consistent speed across the surface. Clean the machine and hoses regularly to avoid clogging.

Hold the spray paint nozzle 6"-8"(15-20cm) away from the surface. Use a spray shield to avoid spraying the surrounding area.

Large areas are difficult to paint with gloss paint as it tends to run. Emulsion is more easily applied. Always spread the paint evenly.

Polyurethane paint does not need the same brushing out as gloss paint. Apply it with a minimum of brushwork and refill the brush as soon as it starts to drag.

Small bubbles can appear when painting over wallpaper. They generally disappear when the paint and wallpaper dry. If they don't, then treat the same as a bubble in wallpaper.

*"The way to get things done is not to mind
who gets the credit for doing them."*

Benjamin Jowett

PAINTING LARGE AREAS

When painting from a paint can, give it a half turn periodically throughout the job. Dip the brush into alternate sides of the can to keep the contents stirred at the surface and prevent a surface film from forming. Occasionally sweep the tip of the brush back and forth through the paint, especially with fast-drying latex paint.

When painting walls roll the first coat on diagonally and the final coat with straight vertical strokes.

Always keep the edges of the roller wet and complete painting a wall before taking a break.

When using a roller cover on several paint jobs, start with the lightest colour and then darker colours, thoroughly cleaning the cover between each job.

For a quicker and more efficient paint job, don't overload the paintbrush or roller. If it drips, there's too much paint.

Keep a damp rag handy to clean up as you go. It's much easier to clean paint when it is still wet.

Prevent splashing a window with paint by wetting a sheet of newspaper and pressing it onto the glass. On frosted glass, paint the glass with neat washing up liquid and wash off with hot water within twelve hours.

To remove dried paint from glass, apply heated vinegar to paint splatters to soften, then scrape off with an old credit card or razor blade.

Paint a ceiling from wall to wall in 2'(60cm) strips, keeping the edges ragged. The edges should be wet when joined.

A water stain will persistently show through emulsion paint. Use a matt oil based paint to cover it first, allow too dry thoroughly before using the emulsion.

Avoid paint from running down your arms when painting a ceiling, cut a slit in a sponge and push the handle of the brush through it. The sponge catches the drips. Wear an old hat so that there's no worry about getting paint on your hair.

Place dishes of water with slices of onion in a room to remove the smell of paint. Other methods are to burn a mixture of charcoal and juniper berries in the room or place a bucket of water with new hay in it. A few drops of lavender oil added to the paint is also very effective.

*"Your future lies before you like a field of driven snow
Be careful how you tread it for every step will show"*

SKIRTING, RADIATORS & PIPES

Use a 2" brush to paint skirtings. A cutting in brush with angled bristles is useful to remove excess paint from corners and crevices.

Use a carpet shield, strips of cardboard or masking tape to stop the paint damaging the carpet. Place the shield under the skirting covering the edge of the carpet. Do not remove until the paint is dry.

Check radiators and pipes for rust before painting. They may need to be primed first.

Do not use metallic paint on radiators as they reduce the heat output. Use radiator enamel paint.

Paint radiators when cold and allow too dry completely before heating.

Do not paint over joints or threads on pipes or radiators as this will make it difficult to unscrew.

Always start at the top of a pipe when painting so that paint drips are caught.

Copper pipes do no require priming, use an undercoat and gloss.

When painting pipes close to a wall use a piece of cardboard as a shield to protect the wall.

Wash, and thoroughly dry plastic gutters and down pipes before painting with gloss paint. Do not use an undercoat.

Prime galvanised metal before painting by scouring it with vinegar. Let the metal dry completely before painting. The paint will go on more easily and not require touching up as often.

Wait a couple of weeks before washing a newly painted surface. Clean with a mild household detergent and a soft cloth.

"Tell a man there are 300 billion stars in the universe, and he'll believe you.
Tell him a bench has wet paint on it, and he'll have to touch to be sure".

EXTERIOR PAINTING

When going to paint the exterior of a house always check the weather forecast. The perfect conditions are 24 hours of mild weather, with little or no humidity and no wind.

Ensure that the early morning dew has cleared before starting to paint and finish well before the evening dew sets in.

During the summer paint the walls after the sun has stopped shining on them and are in shade.

Remove all loose and peeling old paint with a pressure washer. Allow too dry for a day before painting.

Scrape out loose material from cracks and fill with exterior filler. When dry, cover the filler with masonry, water-based, or emulsion paint and allow to dry for 24 hours.

To stop exterior paint peeling in a damp climate, first prime the walls with a breathable oil primer to allow any internal moisture build -up to escape. Paint over the primer with two coats of 100% acrylic latex paint. This will deter mildew and hold its colour.

To avoid future separation between paint coats, the first topcoat should be applied within two weeks after the primer and the second coat within two weeks of the first. As certain paints weather they can form a soap-like substance on their surface which may prevent proper adhesion of new paint coats.

If more than two weeks elapse before applying another paint coat, scrub the old surface with water using a bristle brush or sponge. If necessary, to remove all dirt and deteriorated paint, use a mild detergent. Then rinse well with water, and allow the surface to dry before painting.

Most exterior paints will cover about 400 square feet per gallon for one coat. But adjust for waste factors like the type of surface and equipment used. If the surface is rough or porous, add 20% to the total gallons figured.

It is advisable to buy an extra gallon (5ltr) paint to cover wastage when using rollers or paint sprayers. It is also useful for touching up.

When painting the exterior of a house start at the top and work downwards. Trim, windows and doors should be done last.

"It is a small world, but I wouldn't like to have to paint it."

WALLPAPERING

Make sure new walls are well cured, primed and sized before wallpapering.

Painted walls should have cracks or holes filled and sanded smooth. These areas will need to be primed. If walls are dark coloured and the paper has a light background they should be primed with a white latex primer.

Previously papered walls should have the old paper removed and all old adhesive.

If there is any mould on the old wallpaper it should be treated before stripping. Apply a fungicidal liquid according to the instructions on the bottle, wear gloves and goggles when applying. Leave on for the recommended time then rinse off.

One part household bleach to five parts water can be used to remove mould, leave on for 48 hours before rinsing off.

Lightly score all the old wallpaper in the room, making sure not to damage the plaster beneath. A block of wood with nails set in it protruding slightly will easily score the surface.

When working with water or steam, turn off the power to the electrical appliances in the room to guard against electric shock. Be careful not to allow water to access electrical equipment.

Soak all the wallpaper with warm soapy water with a little wallpaper paste added. Return to starting point and re-soak three sheets of paper. Using a wallpaper scraper, start at the bottom of the first sheet and strip up to the ceiling. Proceed to the next sheet and repeat procedure. Re-soak three more sheets and they will be ready to strip when reached.

Vinyl wallpaper should pull off easily and any backing paper removed as above.

After stripping paper, the walls should be washed down with a mild detergent and a soft bristled scrubbing brush to remove all small bits of paper and old adhesive. Allow too dry before priming or sizing.

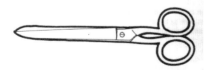

"Ability is what you're capable of doing.
Motivation determines what you do.
Attitude determines how well you do it."

29

WALLPAPERING

Ease the workload when stripping paper by using a steam stripper. Heavy-duty strippers can be hired or purchase a lighter one.

Brush old wallpaper with equal parts of vinegar and water and allow too soak in. For more stubborn areas increase the amount of vinegar.

Loosen the glue on wallpaper borders with a hairdryer.

Wallpaper may be in position for many years so think carefully when choosing a pattern. Striped paper will make a room look higher but the walls must be very straight to use this pattern as any unevenness will be very noticeable.

Make accurate measurements to ascertain the correct number of rolls of paper required. If unsure, check with your supplier or purchase an extra roll.

Standard wallpaper comes in rolls 11yd x 21"(10m x53cm).

Measure the floor to ceiling height not including the skirting. Add 4"(10cm) to the total to allow for trimming.

Measure the circumference of the room. Choose the imperial or metric measurements. As an example of how to calculate the number of rolls required and using imperial measurements for a room 7' high and 30'in circumference - multiply 30' x 12 to convert to 360". Divide 360 x 21(the width of the roll) to find that you will need 17 sheets of paper. Each sheet is 7' long so 17 x 7 equals 119'. Divide by 3 to convert to yards - 39.7. Divide by 11(the length of each roll) and the answer is 4 rolls.

Remember the spacing between the repeats of the pattern will affect the number of rolls required. 10% should be added for wastage when choosing a large pattern.

Rolls of wallpaper are identified by a batch number. Make sure that all rolls required for a job have the same number. Take note of this number for re-ordering extra rolls.

The basic tools required for wallpapering are -
a pair of steps,
bucket for glue and a 6"(15cm) paste brush,
ruler, pencil and a plumb-line,
paper hanging brush or cloth to smooth out the paper,
long-bladed scissors,
a pasting table (A piece of hardboard 6' x 2'(180 x 60cm) on a sturdy frame makes a handy table).

"The reward of a thing well done is to have done it."

It is also useful to have a bucket of soapy water and a rag handy to remove any excess glue from the table.

An angled nail in the end of the paste brush will stop it falling all the way in to the paste can.

To locate screw holes for fixtures when re-papering, place a matchstick or cocktail stick in the rawlplug, protruding slightly. When the paper is brushed down the matchstick will come through the damp paper and show the exact position to refix the screw.

Hanging lining paper serves two functions. Firstly, it provides a smooth even-textured surface, hiding any small blemishes that might show through paint or thin wallpaper. It is particularly useful if the walls have had lots of repairs and filling work. Secondly, it is designed specifically as the perfect base to hang wall covering.

Lining paper under wallpaper should be hung horizontally to ensure that the joints don't coincide with the wall paper joints and also to give maximum bonding strength.

Start wallpapering in an inconspicuous area as this will also be the finishing area and generally the pattern will not match. Areas over doors or windows are usually the best choice.

Work away from the main source of light if possible.

Put the roll of paper against the wall and make a mark a 1/4"(6mm) wider. Using a plumb line and ruler draw a light vertical line the full height of the wall. Use this line as a guide to align the first sheet of paper. If walls are uneven then it may be necessary to draw a plumb line on each wall.

Allow 1-11/4pt(500-700ml) of paste for each roll of paper. Embossed paper will require more.

Sizing walls will help to move the paper into the correct position on the wall without it tearing. It also easier to remove the paper when stripping it at a later stage.

Sizing is a watery mix of glue and water and should be applied to the walls with a paint roller. Allow it to dry before applying the paper.

Always add paste to water instead of water to paste to avoid lumps. Stir the water while adding the paste.

"If at first you don't succeed,
Remove all evidence you ever tried."

WALLPAPERING

To remove small bubbles from new wallpaper, cut a small X over the area. If there is a lump underneath remove the problem with tweezers or the point of a knife. Put some seam adhesive into the opening and squeeze out the excess. Seal the paper down well. Or inject adhesive into the blister and use a seam roller to smooth it.

When applying a patch of wallpaper, tear the paper rather than cutting it. The join will be much less noticeable that way.

After papering steamy rooms such as bathrooms, paint all the joints with clear varnish to prevent peeling.

When hanging vinyl papers, use a special "vinyl to vinyl" adhesive along any overlaps, since vinyl will not stick to itself.

Embossed papers should be handled with care, particularly at joins and corners, to avoid flattening the pattern.

If adding a border over wallpaper do not apply for at least 48 hours after hanging the paper. Borders are glued on with ordinary adhesive.

It is possible to paint over wallpaper providing it is well adhered to the wall with no raised edges. Do not use oil paint.

Always test a small inconspicuous area first as the liquid content of the paint may cause the paper to lift. Sometimes the dyes used to create the pattern in the paper may bleed through new paint. To avoid this, first paint the surface with aluminium sealer.

Do not paint over vinyl paper as this is designed as non-stick.

Previously painted wallpaper may be washed and repainted provided it is sound.

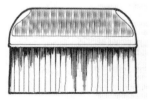

"There are four types of people in this world.
There are people that make things happen.
There are people that watch things happen.
There are people that wonder what happened.
And there are people that don't know anything happened"

THE PLUMBERS MATE

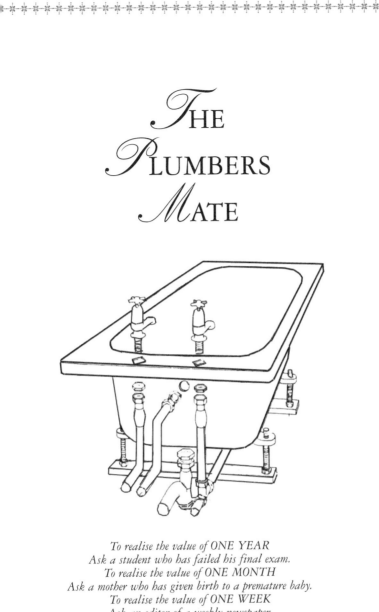

To realise the value of ONE YEAR
Ask a student who has failed his final exam.
To realise the value of ONE MONTH
Ask a mother who has given birth to a premature baby.
To realise the value of ONE WEEK
Ask an editor of a weekly newspaper.
To realise the value of ONE DAY
Ask a daily wage labourer who has ten kids to feed.
To realise the value of ONE HOUR
Ask the lovers who are waiting to meet.
To realise the value of ONE MINUTE
Ask a person who has missed the train.
To realise the value of ONE SECOND
Ask a person who has survived an accident.
To realise the value of ONE MILLISECOND
Ask the person who has won a silver medal in the Olympics.
Treasure every moment that you have!
And treasure it more because you
Share it with someone special
Special enough to have your time

WATER & WASTE

In most houses the cold water supply pipe from the mains supply enters below ground and flows to a storage tank in the roof space through the rising main.

At least one tap, generally in the kitchen, is fed from the rising main.. This provides drinking water.

Pipes from the storage tank distribute cold water to sinks, baths, toilet cisterns and the hot water cylinder.

More pipes distribute hot water from the boiler to the hot water cylinder and then on to baths and sinks.

Waste from baths, sinks and toilets are fed into a soil pipe which is connected at ground level to the drainage system used in any particular area.

The other end of the soil pipe is extended through the roof to prevent foul air from the drainage system contaminating the house.

With so many pipes around in every house it is important to know what to do if a pipe starts to leak.

Outside of each house on the pavement or garden there is an external stop-valve belonging to the local water authority. Turning this valve clockwise will shut off the water to the whole building.

Inside each house there are one or two stop-valves. If there is only one then it will shut off the cold water supply. Where there are two, one will shut off the drinking water supply, the other, generally found in the airing cupboard, will shut off the cold water supply from the storage tank.

It is very important that all household members know where the stop-valves are located and how to turn them off in an emergency.

Open and close all valves at least once a year to check that they are working properly.

If it is difficult to open a stop-valve, apply a little penetrating oil and use a long handled pliers or wrench to give extra leverage.

Always turn off the boiler before draining down the water system.

"Four things drive a man out of his house: too much smoke, a dripping roof, filthy air and a scolding wife"

PLUMBING & PIPES

If there is a water meter periodically check it. When there is no water running in the house all the dials should be stable.

Once a year drain a gallon of water from the drain valve at the base of the hot water cylinder to remove sediment.

Check a metal water storage tank annually for corrosion.

When working in an area where a washer or nut dropped may be difficult to retrieve, use dental floss. Fasten one end of a long piece of floss to the part and the other end to something solid. When the parts are finally installed, the dental floss can either be cut off or, as in the case of a nut, it will come right off because it will be cut by the threading action.

If a new joint feels damp when water is re-admitted to the system, this may just be condensation and not a leak. However check regularly until sure there is no leak.

Instead of using copper pipe and soldered joints for water plumbing, plastic pipes and push-fit joints are easy to assemble, reliable, and can be easily dismantled when necessary.

All pipe work expands when it warms up. Plastic pipe work expands more than copper, so it will need more extra space at the ends. Plastic pipe work is less likely to burst if the water in it freezes and it does not corrode.

To find a leak in a pipe, lather the area with soapy water and bubbles will appear over the hole.

When leaks develop, always inspect the rest of the piping. An entire section may need replacement, especially if the water pressure is low.

At the first sign of a dripping pipe, turn off the water at the mains, turn off the boiler and drain the water system.

A small leak can be temporarily repaired, by rubbing petroleum jelly into the crack and tying a rag tightly around it. Or wrap tightly with plumber's waterproof tape.

A temporary repair to copper piping can be done by cutting a piece of plastic hose 4"(10cm) longer that the crack. Slit the hose and wrap it around the pipe, securing firmly with hose clips.

"We could accomplish a lot more if we'd get rid of our ifs and and's; and get off our butts."

Epoxy resin adhesive will make a more permanent repair. Rub the area with emery paper, mix the resin to the instructions on the tubes and smear it over the crack. Bind the area with plumber's waterproof tape and smear more resin over it. Leave the resin to set according to instructions, before turning on the water.

When turning on water at the mains, leave all the taps open until water starts to come through to prevent airlocks in the system.

If a cold water pipe freezes, turn off the main stopcock and leave the tap on. Thaw the pipe with hot water bottles, a hair-dryer or thick cloths soaked in hot water. Start at the tap end and work backwards.

When water stops coming from the hot tap, turn it off and turn the boiler off immediately as the system is probably drained and the water cylinder can collapse. The frozen pipe is probably the one feeding the tank in the roof-space. Thaw it as above. Let the tank fill before turning on the boiler.

Remember that water expands by one-tenth when frozen so it can crack pipes. When the ice melts the pipes can leak so be prepared with a bucket and cloth when the water is turned on again.

If water is coming out of the tap in spurts then there is probably an airlock in the system. Usually this is the hot tap. First try knocking the pipe gently with a hammer or mallet wrapped in a towel.

If this doesn't work connect a short length of garden hose from hot water tap to the cold water tap with two screw tight rings (Jubilee clips). Turn both taps on full and the mains pressure should force the air out of the system.

When the bottom of a radiator is hot and the top is cool this indicates an airlock. To bleed a radiator, turn off the radiator when it is warm, not hot. Keep a small bowl and rag at hand. Locate the air vent valve at the top of the radiator. Using a radiator key or Allen key turn the screw in an anti-clockwise direction until the air starts to escape. Stop turning immediately as the valve can come out. As soon as the air stops and a trickle of water appears, close the valve. Turn on the radiator and check that it is all hot.

Radiators should not require frequent 'bleeding', if they do then seek professional help.

"Good management is better than good income"

SINKS & TOILETS

Do not use caustic soda to unblock the kitchen sink as it can combine with grease to form a hard substance and block the drain completely.

Sprinkle one cup of washing soda, or a cup of salt and a cup of bicarbonate of soda or a cup of vinegar into the sink outlet. Then pour a kettle of boiling water in to help unblock a sink.

Try clearing the blockage with a plunger. Block the sink overflow with a cloth or tape and if there is a double sink block the second outlet on it as well. Lubricate the rim of the plunger with petroleum jelly and place it over the sink outlet. Half fill the sink with water and pump the plunger up and down several times to create a vacuum and release the blockage. Repeat, if necessary.

If the sink drain is still blocked then place a bowl under the U-bend and undo the trap plug, put a piece of wood or a spanner between the space in the U-bend to steady it. Use a wire coat hanger or flexible curtain wire to prod inside the bend and release any blockage. Grease the threads of the screw with petroleum jelly before replacing and this will make it easier to remove next time.

If the U-bend does not have a drain plug then it will have two screws, undo these and remove it for cleaning.

To stop a toilet overflowing due to an obstruction, remove the tank lid and push the flush valve closed.

A leaky, waterlogged float ball will hold the supply valve open and not completely shut off the water. Flush the toilet, and keep the bar in the cistern held up by hooking to a piece of wood placed across the cistern. This will stop water entering. Unscrew the ball and empty out the water. Dry well and mend any holes with waterproof glue. Replace as soon as possible, with a new float-ball.

If the ball is badly damaged then after removing the water from it, cover with a strong plastic bag long enough to go half way up the bar. Tie the end of the bag securely. This can be used as a temporary measure until a new float is purchased.

Sometimes water deposits build up around the hinge on the bar. Scrape off the deposits and scrub with vinegar.

"Beware of little expenses;
a small leak will sink a great ship"

Benjamin Franklin

If the rod connecting the tank float to the supply valve has become bent, it can prevent the float from reaching its full height, thus leaving the valve open and allowing leakage. This rod should be straightened and a little oil applied to the lever joints to insure smooth action.

If the tank does not fill sufficiently or fill to overflowing, this can be corrected without disturbing the supply valve. Bend the bar attached to the tank float upward or downward. If the rod is bent upward, the water will rise higher in the tank, and if downward, the water level will be lowered.

Sometimes a blocked toilet is caused by a blockage in the toilet bowl and not the drains. To unblock the bowl, pour cold water into the bowl until it is filled to the bottom of the rim. Using a thick mop or the toilet brush with cloths tied around it, plunge the bowl and if the obstruction dislodges, flush the toilet and plunge again.

If the problem is not in the toilet bowl then look into the outdoor inspection trap and check if water is flowing freely from other water outlets. Free flowing water means the problem is in the toilet pipes. Try to dislodge the obstruction by prodding with the handle of a brush or use a discarded length of heavy-duty electrical cable. If this is unsuccessful then call a plumber.

To check if the toilet cistern is leaking, add food colouring to the water and check the bowl after 15-30 minutes.

Beads of moisture on a ceramic cistern are usually caused by condensation. To remedy, improve the room ventilation.

Damaged toilet seats should be replaced rather than repaired. Before purchasing a new seat, measure the size of the bolt holes at the back of the toilet and the distance between the holes.

"There are three ways to obtain wealth:
Inheritance, luck, and hard work.
None is guaranteed,
But you have no influence over the first two."

SHOWERS & BATHS

Often the outlet holes in a shower rose head fills with mineral deposits from the water. Remove the shower rose head and soak it in a bowl of vinegar overnight. Use a needle or a toothpick to clear the holes. Rinse well in cold water and reassemble. Run the shower for a few minutes.

Metal showerheads can be boiled in a mixture of 1/2cup vinegar and 2pt(1tr) water for 15 minutes. Plastic showerheads can be soaked in hot water and vinegar but not boiled.

Scouring powders can damage the surface of baths, basins, sinks and enamel finishes. They contain whiting or pumice and/or silver sand, bleaches, detergents and perfumes.

The easiest way to keep the bath clean is to keep a soft brush and a bottle of thick washing up liquid in the bathroom. After the bath is used, put some washing up liquid on the brush and rub round the tide mark. Rinse well.

A dirty bath and taps can be cleaned with paraffin. Rinse well to eradicate the smell. Or fill the bath with hot water and add a few cupfuls of washing soda. Make sure the crystals are dissolved and leave overnight. Rub with a stiff bath brush and rinse well.

To clean a badly stained bath, use a mix of peroxide and cream of tartar. Make a paste and scrub with a small brush. Rinse thoroughly. If the stain still persists add a drop of ammonia to the mix.

On a lightly stained bath, rub a cut lemon dipped in salt on the stains, rinse off using a soft brush.

If a white enamel bath has yellow stains, rub with a mixture of bicarbonate of soda and turpentine. Leave on for a few hours then rinse well. Repeat, if necessary.

To remove drip marks, rub with warm vinegar and rinse well with hot water. Use daily until the marks disappear. Vinegar is corrosive, so only leave on for a short time.

When resealing around a bath with sealant, put on rubber gloves and dip the fingers in warm, soapy water. Run along the sealant, applying even pressure. This will give an even finish.

Freshly applied bath sealant can be levelled out with an ice cube for a smooth finish.

"One thing you can't recycle is wasted time."

SHOWERS & BATHS

Wash down tiles more easily after using the shower or bath as the steam will have loosened any grime on them.

If tiles are badly stained, make a mixture of bleach and bicarbonate of soda. Brush this onto the tiles and wash off after an hour.

To remove hard water deposit from tiles rub with a cloth dampened with a mixture of equal parts vinegar and water. Polish with a soft dry cloth.

A mouldy shower curtain should be washed with washing powder and bicarbonate of soda added to the water. Soak in a solution of salt water before hanging.

Wash shower curtains in the washing machine with two large bath towels, 1/2 cup detergent and 1/2 cup bicarbonate of soda. Add a cup of vinegar to the rinse cycle. Do not rinse off the vinegar and do not spin dry. Hang up immediately while wet and the wrinkles will disappear as they dry.

To remove build up of grime on shower doors, wipe with lemon oil. Or clean with WD40 spray lubricant.

Shower door tracks will clean easily if the tracks are filled with vinegar and left to soak for several hours. Pour hot water into the tracks to wash away the built up dirt and grime. Use a brush to scrub away any tough spots. For very dirty tracks heat the vinegar in the microwave in a non-reactive pan before pouring into the tracks. This will help loosen the stuck-on grime.

For a non-bleach mildew remover, mix 1 cup white vinegar with 1 cup Borax powder and 2 cups warm water, in a bucket or a spray bottle. Apply to the mildew spot and leave on for 10 minutes. Rinse well.

To make plain glass "frosted" for more privacy, add 1 tablespoon of Epsom Salts to 1 cup of beer. Brush on the window and leave to dry. To remove the frost, wash off with ammonia.

In order that people may be happy in their work,
These three things are needed.
They must be fit for it
They must not do too much of it.
And they must have a sense of success in it.

John Ruskin

SOLDERING

Soft soldering is used where the joined metal is not subject to severe heat or strain. This soldering is done at a low temperature of 120-240oC(250-480oF)

Hard soldering produces a strong joint resistant to stress and strain. This soldering requires a high temperature of 590-900oC(1100-1650oF), generally done with a blowtorch.

Both methods require a soldering alloy and a chemical compound called flux that keeps the joint clean, and helps the solder to flow.

The type of solder and flux used is determined by the metals to be joined and the method used.

Soft solder is an alloy of tin and lead and is available in wire or sticks. Some wire solders have a core of flux that flows with the solder as it melts. This is useful for intricate work.

All-purpose fluxes are available but it is advisable to ask the retailer when purchasing solder what the recommended flux is best for the job in hand.

Soldering irons will produce enough heat for soft soldering. They have a copper tip called a bit and these come in various sizes. These are either heated over a flame or by electricity.

To soft solder a joint, clean the bit and the metal to be repaired. Heat the bit, apply the flux to it and the metal. Melt the solder on the hot bit and holding the join tightly together, draw the soldered bit along the join. Leave to set.

In hard soldering, silver solder with alloys of silver, copper and zinc is used. Brazing uses an alloy of copper and zinc called spelter.

Both solders are available in wires or strips.

The flux used for hard soldering and brazing is borax in either paste or powder form.

When hard core soldering or brazing, the parts to be joined must be heated to an extremely high temperature using a blowtorch.

"Shun idleness.It is a rust that attaches itself to the most brilliant metals."

Voltaire

SOLDERING

To hard solder a joint, clean the metal parts to be joined with a file or emery cloth. Coat with the flux. Clamp the join together securely and heat with a blowtorch until the metal glows. Lay the solder along the joint heating continuously with the blowtorch.

Leave the solder to cool and set. Wash off the flux with hot water and rub the joint with a fine flat file.

Safety is very important when soldering. Never allow children near solder irons.

Always use a secure soldering iron stand and never leave soldering irons plugged in when not in use. Work in a well-ventilated area.

After each soldering session, unscrew the iron tip slightly to keep it from fusing to the barrel of the iron.

If solder spits and spurts when soldering, you may be using too much flux.

For neat solder seams avoid stopping or starting the solder line at a joint..

Staple a piece of steel wool to the work-bench and use this to regularly clean the tip of the solder iron.

Wrap a length of solder wire around the electric cord of the solder iron to have it easily accessible when required. Or clip a length of solder wire to the iron with a large bulldog clip.

A solder joint should take hold in a few seconds, otherwise it is not going to hold.

The smallest speck of dirt or the tiniest trickle of running water along the area to be soldered will prevent the joint taking hold.

When soldering a water pipe, prevent water trickling by stuffing a wad of bread into the pipe to absorb the water, remove before it dissolves. Use white bread; whole grains can get caught in valves.

Good soldering is a skill that is learnt by practice. The most important point in soldering is that both parts of the joint to be made must be at an equal high temperature. This allows the solder to flow evenly and make a good join.

"Where there is a will there is a way."

Soldered joints may stay hot for a long time afterwards.

Make sure that no parts of the joint move after the soldering iron is removed and until the solder is completely hard. This can take quite a few seconds with large joints. If the joint is disturbed during this cooling period it may become seriously weakened.

Hard cold solder will have a smooth shiny appearance and on a properly made joint the bond should be very strong.

It is important to use the correct amount of solder, both on the iron and on the joint. Too little solder on the iron will give poor heat transfer to the joint and too much will allow the solder to form strings as the iron is removed, causing splashes to other contacts. Too little solder applied to the joint will only give a good bond where the soldering iron has been and none on the rest of the joint.

Remember it is much more difficult to correct a poorly made joint than it is to make the joint properly in the first place.

Paint anti-flux on an area to stop solder flowing into it. Ordinary toothpaste can be used in an emergency.

When soldering two wires together, heat the solder over a hard surface and let the drops fall. Shape the flat circles around the two pieces of twisted wires. Reheat the circles and the solder will melt around the wire.

Soldering a pipe can be difficult. Wrap the section to be soldered tightly with copper wire, extending the area by 1/4"(6mm) on each side. The solder will flow around the wire and have a better bond.

To solder a narrow seam, first tape two crayons together and run these along the line, with the two marks straddling the line to be soldered. Any excess solder will be removed when the crayon is scraped off.

Wash off all the burnt flux when the work is completed.

When mending tiny holes in a bucket or tank, place a light under the container and this will show where to apply the solder.

Use magnets or plasticine to hold small parts in place when soldering.

*"Don't throw away the old bucket until you know
whether the new one holds water."*

HELPFUL HINTS

When working on replacing a tap head always insert the plug in the sink or bath so that no small parts are lost.

Use grips to tighten compression fittings.

When using an oversized spanner to unscrew a small nut, place a coin between jaw and nut.

A temporary repair for a split copper pipe is to place a matchstick over the dry split, pour on hot wax and tape up.

Increase the heat from radiators by pasting strong aluminium foil behind the radiator.

When carrying a heavy bucket the wire handle can be uncomfortable on the hand, take an open-ended spanner and let the bucket handle run through each end of the spanner. Pick up the bucket with the spanner.

To mend a small hole in a galvanised watering can, seal it with enamel paint.

To avoid the liquid contents of large cans with screw on lids from running down the side of the can, keep the hole at the top when pouring. This allows air to enter the can and the liquid will pour steadily.

Small flat cans will the hole in the centre should be held with the longest sides of the can horizontal.

Use lengths of scrap iron pipe as rollers underneath heavy objects to be moved. Put a length under the front and back of the object and 2-4 more in between depending on the size. As the object moves, put the pipe that comes out the back at the front. To change direction put the pipe lengths at the required angle.

Dip a pad of steel wool in paraffin and use to remove stubborn rust stains from metal.

Use an old clipboard to hold sheets of sandpaper. Put a piece of strong cardboard on top to stop the sheets from curling up. Or clip them to the bottom of the board with a large bulldog clip.

Wet steel wool will rust quickly, store it in a cup of water with 1tsp of bicarbonate of soda added.

"The trouble with doing something right the first time is that nobody appreciates how difficult it was"

AN
ELECTRIC
CURRENT

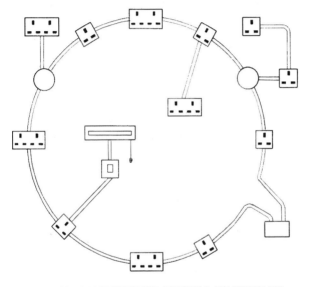

EVENTUALLY EVERY DAY WILL BE SUNDAY

Every year has 365 days.
If you sleep eight hours a day it equals 122 days.
This leaves 243 days.
If you rest eight hours a day it equals another 122 days.
This leaves 121 days.
There are 52 Sundays.
This leaves 69 days.
If you have a half-day on Saturday, this equals 26 days.
This leaves 43 days.
Taking a 11/2 hour lunch on work days, equals 28 days.
This leaves 15 days.
Two weeks vacation equals 14 days.
This leaves only one day.
On Labour Day nobody works.

ELECTRIC SAFETY

Never attempt to do anything with electricity, gas or other services unless you know exactly what you are doing. Inexperienced fiddling can be very dangerous.

Water and electricity don't mix. Even when carrying out harmless tasks such as washing down walls, turn off the electricity first. Never use any wet electrical plugs, sockets or equipment, unless you are sure that they have thoroughly dried out.

To prevent yourself from getting electric shocks, first check that your neon test screwdriver is working by touching a live terminal. Then before commencing any electrical work apply the screwdriver to each terminal.

Extension cables often need to be uncoiled before use, or they could overheat - check the instructions. Make sure that it is safe to use the extension cable with an appliance before you start.

If an extension cord gets tangled up, don't pull on the ends. Instead, gently loosen all the tighter snarls in the middle until they become larger loops that can easily be untangled. A way to avoid tangles is to use a retractable cord reel. It will let you reel out only the amount of cord required, then quickly reel it back when finished.

When wiring a workshop, install extra outlets in the ceiling, positioned over groupings of power tools. Ceiling outlets can be more accessible and can help eliminate tripping over extension cords. Also plan to install at least one outlet every 3'(1m) around the perimeter.

If you can't avoid working with electrical appliances in damp conditions, you should use a power breaker. This automatically cuts off the power supply in the case of an accident (such as a cut cable) or a malfunction.

Take care not to use too many plugs or adapters on an electrical socket - it could overload Where feasible, check that the connections inside each plug are tight. Ensure that the cord grip is tightened around the cable rather than the wires inside the cable.

When fixing or checking electrical appliances or connections, always switch off the power and remove the fuse or circuit breaker. If you're fixing an electrical appliance, switch it off at the socket and pull out the plug. Wear rubber-soled shoes when working with electric.

"An ounce of prevention is worth a pound of cure."

WIRES & FUSES

Wiring that falls out of its routing on equipment has a tendency to get torn off. Metal clips help to solve this problem, but another solution is to use silicone caulk. Put a dab where the wire is to run, then push the wiring into the dab. Tape the wire lightly so it stays put while the silicone cures.

A poor electrical contact can get very hot when a high current is flowing. A common cause of poor contacts in junction boxes and switch boxes is for the conductor to be trapped alongside the terminal screw rather than clamped down by the screw. Usually a really good tug on the cable will reveal any bad contacts of this sort.

When moving into a new house find out which fuses control the various parts of the house. To find out which fuse controls which circuit, first number each fuse then turn on all the lights. Switch off the main switch in the fuse box and pull out the first fuse. Switch on the main switch and take note of which lights, socket outlets or fixed appliances are not working. Switch off the main switch, replace the fuse and then repeat the procedure with the remaining fuses.

Keep these notes, spare fuses and a selection of fuse wire, a small electrical screwdriver, a candle and a lighter or matches in a bag attached to the door of the fuse box.

The grades of fuse wire are:-
Thin wire 5 amp for lighting
Thicker wire 15 amp for immersion heaters and other 3kw circuits
20 amp for some types of water heaters
30 amp for ring circuits
Very thick 45 amp for cookers.

Before replacing a blown fuse wire locate the faulty appliance, lead or overloaded circuit that caused the problem and disconnect.

To replace a fuse wire, switch off the main switch. Take out the fuses one at a time to find the one that has blown (the wire will have snapped). Loosen the terminal screws and remove the old wire. Wrap one end of the new wire around one terminal and tighten. Pull the wire to the other terminal and wind around it in an anti-clockwise direction. Tighten the screw. Trim off any surplus wire and replace the fuse. Switch on the main switch.

"Enthusiasm is the electricity of business"

WIRES & FUSES

Ensure that cables, flexes, plugs and bulbs are the correct amp rating for the circuits and appliances they are being used for.

Never use a fuse with a higher amp than required. 3 amp fuses are used for appliances of up to 700 watts (electric blankets, power tools, standard or table lamps and stereos), 13 amp fuses are generally used for all other appliances.

Do not ignore a fishy smell in a room. Check all plugs or electrical appliances that are switched on. One of them could be overheating and burning the plastic.

Never touch electrical equipment with wet hands and do not use electrical equipment in the bathroom. The only safe exceptions are a razor with a two-pin plug working from a razor socket, a pull cord switch for the light bulb and pull cord switch for electric showers.

When using an electric drill in the bathroom connect it to an extension lead plugged in outside the bathroom.

Check plugs and flexes often for wear and tear. Fix loose connections immediately and never allow a flex to become frayed or worn.

If the wires are not damaged, a frayed flex can be temporarily repaired with insulating tape but it is important to replace it with a new flex as soon as possible.

Avoid running cables under carpets as they can get damaged and the wires become exposed.

When hammering nails into a wall always check where the electric cables run (also water and gas pipes).

When wiring a basic plug hold the plug upright with the pins away from you. The bRown wire goes to the right (live terminal marked L), the bLue wire to the left (neutral terminal marked N) and the third wire, green and yellow,(earth terminal marked E) goes in the centre.

To save small parts during a project, use small plastic bags. Throw the parts in the bag and tack it up on the wall. If not completing the job immediately all the parts will be kept safely. This is especially useful while doing electrical work. Put receptacle screws and covers in a bag and tack it up next to the outlets.

"Looking for new ways to do old jobs means progress."

To prevent a power tool lead coming apart from an extension cable while working, loop the leads together as if making a knot, Instead of completing the knot plug them together and this will make them unable to be unplugged.

When rewiring a lamp it can be difficult to get the new cord up the small pipe. The easiest way is to tie a string to the end of the old cord before removing it, pull the old cord out and attach the string to the new cord to pull it through.

Lay electrical wires separate from computer or cable wires. The household current carried through electrical wires can cause interference in other cables. They should be kept at least 4"(10cm) apart and never tie them together. If they need to cross, keep them at right angles.

Use the inner cardboard tubes from tin-foil or cling film rolls to stop computer or cable wires getting tangled. Loop the surplus wire loosely and insert into the tube neatly.

Never use water to extinguish a fire in an electrical appliance. Keep a chemical fire extinguisher in the house for this purpose.

Unplug electronic equipment that is rarely used. In the average home, 75% of all electricity used to power home electronics is consumed while products are turned off.

Batteries will keep their charge longer if they're kept cool. Warmer temperatures will shorten their life.

Always recharge a battery immediately after it is used. Never store an uncharged battery and recharge unused batteries every two months.

Energy-saving bulbs are good in lights that tend to be left on for extended periods of time, such as exterior lights. Energy-saving bulbs typically use 75% less energy than standard bulbs, and they'll last up to 10 times longer with reduced costs over time.

Before installing a rooftop antenna or satellite dish, make sure it is away from any power lines. It's best to locate antennas and dishes where they won't touch or fall on electrical lines if they happen to be blown off. Also, be sure to properly ground them to avoid any electrical damage to the home or appliances.

"The way to develop self-confidence is to do the thing you fear to do and get a record of successful experiences behind you."

Dale Carnegie

ELECTRICITY IN THE HOME

The local electricity board generates electricity into homes by a service cable to a sealed fuse unit.

The live wire supply has a red sheath while the neutral has black. The bare wire is the earth and it is connected from the casing of the fuse box to the ground.

Never attempt to open the sealed fuse unit.

The live and neutral wires run from the sealed fuse box through an electricity board meter. This records the amount of electricity used.

The total amount of electricity that can be used at any one time is determined by the rating of the electricity board's sealed fuse and also the type of wiring used.

In older houses the power distribution around the home may have a radial wiring system.

This means that all power sockets are supplied from one fuse box with a mains switch. There are separate fuse boxes, each with a mains switch, for lighting circuits and for heavy usage equipment such as immersion heaters or cookers.

Newer installations will have ring-mains wiring.

In this case there is usually only one fuse box and one mains switch. Many or all of the wall sockets are connected by a continuous single loop of cable, called a ring circuit. Generally one ring serves the upstairs power sockets while another one will supply the ground floor.

There are separate fuses and circuits for lighting circuits and heavy usage equipment.

Spurs or branch cables are connected to the ring cable to supply outlying sockets. If heavy usage equipment is used on a spur, less power is available to other sockets on the ring.

New circuits or spur cables from an existing ring should be installed by a qualified electrician.

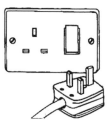

"A helping hand is no further than at the end of your sleeve."

$\mathscr{I}$NVALUABLE $\mathscr{T}$OOLKIT

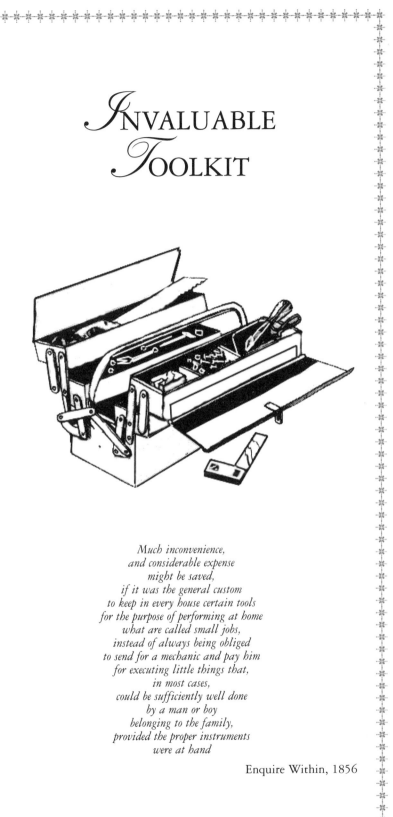

Much inconvenience,
and considerable expense
might be saved,
if it was the general custom
to keep in every house certain tools
for the purpose of performing at home
what are called small jobs,
instead of always being obliged
to send for a mechanic and pay him
for executing little things that,
in most cases,
could be sufficiently well done
by a man or boy
belonging to the family,
provided the proper instruments
were at hand

Enquire Within, 1856

"The frog does not drink up the pond in which he lives."

TOOLS

When it comes to buying tools, don't compromise on quality. Inexpensive tools may seem like a bargain at the shop, but will be disappointing in their performance.

Acquire tools as you need them. Avoid buying tools you will never use.

Choose tools that feel comfortable in your hand. Examine them for sturdiness and check moving parts for smoothness when working.

Always keep tools clean and lubricated, store them out of the way and in a dry place when not in use.

Handle tools with care, throwing them into a tool-box can dull or nick the edges and make them difficult to find.

If possible hang up tools with cutting edges separately and keep power tools and their accessories in carrying cases.

The normal dulling of the cutting edge of a tool can be corrected with an oilstone. This is called honing. Double-sided stones with a coarse side for rubbing down and a fine side to keen the edge are useful.

When sharpening the blade of a tool on an oilstone, move evenly over the whole surface to avoid forming groves. Apply light oil to the stone to keep the stone smooth.

Electric powered bench grinders can be used to sharpen tools. They have fine and coarse wheels. The grinding is usually done dry and fast but be careful that the tool doesn't become overheated resulting in a loss of hardness to the cutting edge.

Apply only light pressure to the tool when grinding and frequently dip it in a bucket of water to avoid overheating.

Keep a few mothballs or packets of silica gel in the toolbox to absorb damp and prevent the tools from rusting. A magnet is also useful to keep small screws together.

When working with certain timbers and steel tools for lengthy periods the hands can develop a dark purple/black staining. To remove - wash the hands with lemon juice.

Keep a pair of goggles safely on the workbench in an old cotton sock, it stops them getting scratched.

"It's the tools a man uses, not the tools he may possess, that make his profit."

MEASURING TOOLS

A retractable steel tape measure 16' - 33'(5-10m) is very useful. If the tape is 1"(2.5cm) wide, it will be safer and easier to use. The play in the hook allows either inside or outside measurements to be made without having to compensate for the hook. Its flexibility allows it to measure round, contours, and other odd-shapes. When making inside measurements, add the measurement of the tape case, usually marked on the case. Check for flexibility and how fast it retracts.

To keep a retracting tape measure in good condition, wipe the metal tape with a dab of car wax, then wipe with a clean cloth. This will help protect the tape's finish and keep it retracting smoothly.

Tape measures are great for determining distance but a thick metal rule is better for marking. Hold it on its side to eliminate any viewing angle distortion and strike off the measurements with a hard leaded pencil. For even greater accuracy, score the mark with a utility knife and get a start to the cut.

Squares are used for laying out work, checking that it is square and marking angles. The better types have a number of tables, conversions, and formulas stamped on the side to simplify many woodworking tasks.

A straight edge is a rigid, flat steel or wooden bar with one bevelled edge. They are usually one metre in length. They can be used to draw straight lines or as a guide for a knife or blade when cutting veneers.

Chalk-line is a string or line coated with coloured chalk used to transfer a straight line to a working surface easily and accurately. Pull the line out and hold it tight between the two points of measurement Then snap it to leave a mark. Some have a pointed case to double as a plumb bob.

Levels are used to make sure work is true horizontal (level) or true vertical (plumb). Always use the longest level possible. The torpedo level is 8"-9"(20-22cm) in length, with vials that read level, plumb, and 45 degrees. It is used for small pieces of work. A 2'-4'(60-100cm) level is essential for any woodworking project.

"A try angle will take you round the hardest of corners."

MEASURING TOOLS

To know if a level is true, place it on a flat surface making sure the bubble is exactly in the centre and mark off the ends of the level. Flip the level once over within the same marks. If the level is accurate, the bubble should still be in the same position. Finally switch the ends of the level. If the bubble stays centred it is ready to use.

When using a long metal level or rule on a smooth wall, stop it slipping by gluing small squares of glass-paper on the sides of the level with rubber cement. These can be easily removed when not required.

A plumb bob is a heavy, balanced weight on a string, which is dropped from a specific point to locate another point exactly below it, or to determine true vertical.

A good carpenter measures twice and cuts once. Accuracy and care in measuring are all important. It can mean a well-put-together project or a sloppy one.

When marking out, especially with multiple cuts from one piece, always allow for the width of the saw cut.

Measurements can be marked in various ways, depending on how accurate they need to be. A felt-tipped pen or an ordinary hard lead pencil with a well-sharpened point are easily read, and can be used where accuracy is not too critical. A carpenter's pencil is more accurate and gives easy-to-read measurements.

When many pieces need to be cut and/or drilled to the same measurement, use one accurately cut or drilled piece as a template to mark all the others. However, for greatest accuracy, always rely on a tape measure or rule.

Even on rough carpentry projects, such as laying out a wall or partition with a carpenter's square, sharpen the pencil after every six marks. To keep the pencil point sharp, rub it back and forth a few times against a sanding sheet. This will give the pencil point a chisel shape that is excellent for marking.

Most products are sold in metric quantities, but some are still in the imperial system. Always work in one system only - changing between the two is confusing and often inaccurate. Tapes and rules are usually marked in both systems of measurement.

"If a man measures life by what others do for him,
he is going to be very disappointed."

Always allow a margin for wastage and error when calculating materials. This can save time rather than having to re-order or spoil the job by skimping.

When marking to cut very fine work, use a marking knife or a craft knife. These not only mark, but also cut the fibres very slightly to enable further cutting to be very exact.

The simplest way to divide work equally is to hold the rule diagonally across the surface and decide how many divisions are required. Make sure that the end of the rule is level with the edge of the material and the divisions will fall equal automatically.

Use retractable rules with care as they can sometimes snap back quickly.

When marking with a knife, keep fingers away from the blade, and don't apply excessive pressure. Keep the knife at a constant angle.

Put a strip of masking tape on the ruler to write down measurements, discard when finished with it.

When measures or gauges on stamped metal tools become difficult to read, rub a crayon with a contrasting colour over the area. Then rub lightly with a cloth dampened in turpentine, the surface crayon rubs off but the remainder will stay in the stamped area. Coat with clear varnish to seal.

Mark measurements for transfer on a metal ruler with a small magnet. On a wooden ruler clasp a plastic electric tie or a band of metal around the ruler and slide along the ruler as required.

To see marks more clearly on a carpenter's rule, wipe with a soft rag dipped in white paint.

Approximate conversions
Square metres to square yards	add one fifth
Acres to hectares	multiply by 2 and divide by 5
Hectares to acres	multiply by 5 and divide by 2
Kilometres to miles	divide by 10 and multiply by 6
Miles to kilometres	divide by 6 and multiply by 10

"They who commit a mistake and do not correct it, commit another mistake."

SCREWDRIVER

Screwdriver sets have a selection of range of sizes of flat and cross-head bits.

When using a cross head screwdriver the tip must fit exactly into the cross on the screw or it will slip.

Short-bladed screwdrivers are useful for work in confined spaces.

Multi-bit screwdrivers are very convenient to have. Tips can either be stored within the driver handle or have interchangeable bits in the unit.

Electrical screwdrivers are used to work with plugs and electrical appliances. The handle is insulated in heavy-duty plastic. The safest electric screwdriver has the blade insulated in a plastic sleeve and a gauge for registering an electric current.

The Philips head screwdriver is designed to reduce blade slippage. It has a single blade and is used with screws of matching heads.

Rechargeable battery or cordless screwdrivers have changeable blades and are very versatile.

Magnetic tipped screwdrivers are very handy for holding onto smaller screws, especially in tight places. Magnetise screwdrivers by running a magnet down the blade five or six times in one direction only. To demagnetise it, run the magnet in the opposite direction.

A piece of pipe insulation wrapped around a screwdriver handle will give a better grip when more torque is required, or when the handle is slippery.

When using a screwdriver, always try to match the size of the screwdriver blade to the size of the screw as closely as possible. Mismatches will frequently result in the screw stripping and excessive wear on the screwdriver blade resulting in a more difficult and time-consuming job.

To keep a screwdriver from slipping, rub chalk on the blade.

A screwdriver may look like a pry bar, chisel or punch, but it should never be used for such purposes A screwdriver works best when the blade is straight, balanced, and sharp. The handle should be clean and free of oil or grease.

"Keep a thing for seven years and you'll find a use for it."

HAMMERS

A good quality hammer will be forged from carbon steel using a specialised hardening and tempering process that produces a hammerhead with a tough striking surface.

The handle should be made of hickory or ash as these woods are tough and long grained, and able to withstand the strain exerted on them in the course of normal use.

Carpenter's hammer - there are two types, the claw hammer with a curved claw, used for pulling nails or a ripping hammer with a straight claw that fits easily between boards. The claw on the ripping hammer can also be used to pull nails. Both hammers will have wood, steel or fibreglass handles and come in a variety of face styles and weights.

The Warrington hammer or joiner's hammer is used for lighter work. The end of the hammer opposite the striking face has a narrow striking edge that is very useful for driving tacks or small nails. Sometimes they have magnetic heads.

Club hammers or lump hammers are used to strike short heavy blows when breaking holes in walls or solid floors.

Mallets are used for hitting other objects like chisels or to beat sheet metal. They are usually made from beech wood and benefit from an occasional soaking in linseed oil.

Sledge hammers are used for heavy work on concrete or for hitting a wedge when splitting wood.

To securely install a new handle on a hammer, coat the end of the handle with epoxy glue before inserting into the hammerhead.

To temporarily tighten a loose hammer handle, pull a piece of wire gauze over the end of the handle before re-inserting. Take care when using tools with loose heads as they can easily fly off.

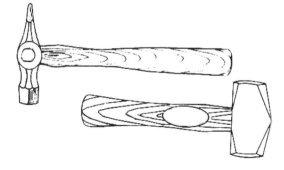

*"The mason who strikes often
is better than the one who strikes too hard."*

HAMMERS

To tighten a hammer handle, soak it in used engine oil for a day.

Bent nails can be the result of bad hammering technique or by a dirty hammer face. Occasionally rub the hammer face with fine sandpaper.

Practice hammering nails into a scrap piece of wood.

Effective control of a hammer lies in the handle. The handle increases the force of the swing and so determines the impact on the nail head. Use the wrist and not the elbow to swing the hammer.

Protect the work surface when hammering a nail by cutting a slit in a piece of inner rubber tube and inserting it around the nail. Drive in the nail until it reaches the tubing, remove the tubing and a further hammer tap will put the nail fully in.

A rounded hammerhead face is ineffective when hammering nails. Put the head in a vice and file the face until it is flat.

When hitting hand tools with a claw hammer turn the hammer on it's side and there is less chance of hitting your hand.

The claw of a hammer is used to remove nails. Insert the claw under the nail head and pull. For long protruding nails, place a piece of scrap wood under the claw to protect the surface beneath from being damaged when prising out the nail.

When using a claw hammer to remove very tough nails, slip a length of steel pipe over the head of the hammer. This creates a V-shaped tool allowing the use of both hands to work the claw.

When hitting wooden handled hand tools use a wooden mallet.

Use safety goggles when hammering metals. Chips can fly from steel chisels or nail heads break off.

To store a sledge hammer, 1"(2.5cm) from the end of the handle opposite the head, drill a hole crosswise and hang up with the head flat against the wall.

*" You can fool some of the people all the time,
and all the people some of the time,
but you can't fool all of the people all the time."*

SAWS

Panel or crosscut saws are used to cut across the grain of wood. They have small, offset teeth. An 8-point saw is best for general use. The more teeth they have the finer the cut.

Rip saws cut with the grain, and have much larger teeth.

Combination saws cut both across and with the grain.

Hacksaws are used on metal, plastic and electrical conduit. They have thin, removable blades that should be renewed frequently.

Coping saws are required to follow an irregular, delicate, or intricate cut in wood. The blade is thin, fine toothed, and removable.

Fret saws are for cutting tight curves in wood plastic and glass fibre. They can only be used on light work.

Pad or keyhole saws have a blade that is narrower at the tip than at the heel or handle. It is used for cutting openings in drywall or panelling or for curved cuts for keyholes.

The mitre saw is a very versatile and accurate tool. The blade can pivot over the base to get the exact angle required, and each successive piece cut, will have the same angle. This is very useful for mouldings and frames. It can shave small amounts off to adjust the cut until it is perfect.

Electric circular saws are used for straight cutting of timber, man-made boards, laminated and plastic boards, sheet metal, thicker softer metals, masonry and ceramic tiles.

A circular saw consists of: -
a replaceable blade;
a blade guard, part of which is spring loaded to move out of the way as you saw;
a sole plate, which may or may not be attached to it;
a ripping fence;
a cutting guide and knobs to adjust the cutting angle and depth of the blade.

Set the cutting depth to 1/8" more than the thickness of the board. Avoid binding by keeping the sole plate flat on the surface of the wood.

"Leisure is sweet when it follows work well done."

SAWS

Never use the wrong type of blade in a circular saw. Always match the type and rpm rating of blade to the material being cut.

Before and after each use, check the saw's safety mechanisms. Make sure that blade guards are operating properly and smoothly. When the blade's at full speed, push the saw forward smoothly without forcing it.

To protect the teeth of a circular saw blade, when not in use, cut a 1"(2.5cm) band from a tyre tube and stretch it over the teeth.

Electric jig-saws or sabre saws are used to cut straight or curved cuts in timber, metals and various other materials by using different blades. They have a small blade that cuts with an up and down motion. A good quality saw will have a long stroke and about 3000 strokes per minute.

When starting to cut a circle in a piece of material, drill a starting hole, to allow the blade to enter. Many models have a circle guide, angle cutting and ripping accessories.

Do not start a saw motor with the blade touching the work piece. Let the motor reach full speed before it begins the cut.

A hacksaw is the perfect tool to make a quick smooth cut in a metal pipe. Use both hands while cutting and hold the saw on both ends. Apply firm pressure on the push strokes, and lift up slightly on the blade on the return strokes. This should give a nice smooth cut.

If a hacksaw is required to cut through a fastened pipe or rod, but the space above is cramped. Remove the hacksaw's blade, straddle the pipe with its frame from below and reinstall the blade upside down. The teeth of the saw will cut through the pipe from the opposite side.

To cut a wider slot with a hacksaw put two blades together. Parallel cuts can be made, by placing a small spacer between the two blades.

Make a small useful saw with a broken hacksaw blade by wrapping one end of the blade with tape to use as a handle.

To make sawing easier, rub the blade of a saw with paraffin, a candle, a bar of soap, or use shaving-cream as it does not stain.

*"A sharp tongue is the only edged tool
that grows keener with constant use."*

Washington Irving

When sawing wood, consider which side of the material to have facing up. Keep the good side up when using hand-saws, scroll saws, band-saws, table-saws and radial-arm saws. Keep the good side down when using a portable circular saw or saber saw. The principle is to have the tooth of the blade first break through the rough side of the board or panel.

To saw easily let the saw do the work. Do not use too much force, instead use as much of the saw's length as possible and only press on the saw stroke away from you. Try to saw with a steady rhythm.

Rip cuts go with the woodgrain. After exact measurement and marking have been made, carefully use the thumb to guide the saw with two or three short upward strokes. Once the cut has started, hold the saw at a 60 degree angle to the wood and use smooth, full down strokes.

When cutting a long piece of board, stop the wood binding the saw and making it difficult to move by putting a wedge of wood in the saw cut to keep it open.

To cut a piece of wood thicker than the cut of the saw blade, use a carpenter's square to mark matching cuts on opposite sides of the timber. Then set the saw's thickness guide to just over half the width of the piece you want to cut. Cut twice, once on each side for a perfect cut all the way through.

When wood to be cut is veneered on both sides, mark the cutting line on the underside and score through it with a sharp blade before sawing. This prevents splinters of the veneer from chipping off.

When cutting plywood put a strip of masking tape along the cut line to have a clean, cut edge with no splinters.

Gum or resin on a saw blade can be easily removed with oven-cleaner. Wearing gloves and goggles, spray on the cleaner and leave for the required time according to the instruction on the tin. Wipe off and rinse well. Drill bits can be cleaned in the same way using an old toothbrush.

Put a length of hose over the teeth of hand saws to protect them or cut a piece of 1"(2.5cm) tongue-and groove flooring the length of the saw. Place the saw blade in the groove, secure the saw to the wood with thick rubber bands.

When choosing blades for an electric saw, steel blades are less expensive but dull easily. Carbide-tipped blades are more expensive but will last longer.

CLAMPS, PLIERS & SPANNERS

Clamps are for holding objects together while they are being worked on or while various adhesives are drying.

C-clamps are the most common. So named because of their shape, they have swivel heads that make the clamps self-aligning for odd-shaped pieces.

Bar clamps are useful for clamping extra-wide work.

A vice is a workbench tool and should be firmly secured before being used. It is used for holding work being sawed, bored, glued, or formed in some way.

General purpose pliers have a variety of uses from bending to pulling objects and cutting wire.

Long-nosed pliers are useful in confined spaces.

Carpenter's pincers remove nails and tacks.

The jaws of pliers are made for gripping and can leave marks on material. To avoid this either, cover the jaws with masking tape or cut the fingers from an old pair of gloves and pull these over the jaws.

Open-ended spanners come in a variety of sizes and are used to open nuts and bolts or for working on pipes.

When an open-ended spanner will not grip a worn nut, get the next larger size and insert the blade of a screwdriver into the gap. The flat screwdriver blade will give the spanner more leverage.

If a spanner is slightly too large to fit around an object, wrap a thin strip of lead around the object to make it fit.

Adjustable spanners are particularly useful for plumbing work.

Since the fixed jaw of an adjustable spanner is the strongest side, it is sensible when using the spanner to apply the force so it works mainly against the stronger jaw.

Monkey wrenches lock on to objects so that they are very firmly gripped but they can heavily mark the object.

"It's no delay to stop to edge the tool."

CHISELS, PLANES & FILES

Bevelled-edge chisels have a tapered edge and are useful for working in small spaces.

Cold chisels are used to chip off ceramic tiles or remove mortar from brickwork.

Bolster chisels are used to lever up objects like floorboards.

A chisel is a very useful tool, but it's important to know how to use it. For example, after routing out a mortise for a door hinge, use the flat side of the chisel for cutting or to neaten the edges, and the bevelled side for cleaning up or levelling a surface without taking off too much at a time.

To chisel, start the blade digging into the wood slightly inside the guideline mark. Do not cut too deeply, chisels are meant to chip and shave away. Put the bevelled edge into the work so that it constantly directs the chisel out of the wood for better control. Keep the cutting edge directed away from you body and hands.

Never begin sanding on the wood of any carving project until it is completed. The small particles of abrasive that lodge in the grain can dull carving tools fast, and can quickly destroy all the benefits of using good sharpening equipment and techniques.

Planes are for removing very thin layers of wood, for trimming and smoothing, for straightening or bevelling edges or for adding a groove.

Plane with the grain of the wood whenever possible, to avoid catching and lifting chips of wood.

Prevent splitting the corners on material you are planing by clamping scraps of wood on either side of the corner at the same level.

Always keep blades razor sharp.

When it's not in use, rest the plane on its side to avoid dulling the blade.

Using a hand plane on the ends of boards can be tricky. One way to keep from splitting a board at the edges is to push the hand plane so the blade goes only to the middle of the board. Then repeat the process from the other direction.

*"There is a keystone to every arch,
and a combination to every lock."*

CHISELS, PLANES & FILES

To avoid dipping, try to put slightly more pressure on the front of the plane at the beginning of each stroke, and keep slightly more pressure on the back of the plane at the end of the stroke.

Files are used for shaping. They are shaped round, half-round, flat, square, and triangular. Single-cut file teeth run in one direction, double-cut teeth run in opposite directions. The latter will cut more coarsely, but quicker.

Rasps differ from files in that the teeth are formed individually, not connected to one another. Generally a longer file or rasp will have coarser teeth than a shorter one. Files will cut smoother than rasps, but, when used on wood, will work much slower and are susceptible to clogging.

Files with an attachable handle are easier to use.

When using hand files, it is best to hold the work piece firmly in a vice or clamp.

For better results, try to keep the piece being filed at about elbow height for general filing. For heavier filing work, the piece should be lower; if the work is finer or delicate try to keep it up closer to eye level.

Files should always be protected from grease, water, or nicks that can make them less effective. When carrying files in a toolbox, it is a good idea to wrap them in a cloth.

Keep file teeth clean by using a wire brush, working along the grain, to clear the grooves.

Roll a small ball of putty over the surface of a file to remove small particles from between the teeth.

Stick a piece of masking tape over the file, rub the tape to press it into the file. When the tape is peeled off it will remove any particles lodged in the teeth.

When filing aluminium, dip the file in paraffin to stop filings getting stuck in the teeth. Or rub blackboard chalk over the file to stop metal particles sticking to it.

When storing files, try to hang them in a rack, keep them in a drawer with wooden divisions or store files in protective sleeves to stop the teeth from dulling.

"Neither a borrower nor a lender be."

Drills

A single-speed drill is only useful for light work like drilling holes in wood.

A cordless drill eliminates the need for cumbersome extension cords and can be used where power is not available.

Two or three speed drills can be used for light or heavy work especially if they have a hammer action. More versatile drills can be fitted with sanding or other attachments

When using a two-speed drill allow to stop before changing speed.

Frequently check the air filters on tools. Clogged filters can choke an engine and many filters can be cleaned and reused

When using a drill apply steady pressure in line with the axis of the drill. Too little pressure can cause excessive friction at the tip of the drill. Sideways pressure can cause the drill bit to snap inside the hole.

When drilling ensure that the work is secured firmly to avoid damage to either it or the drill.

Unplug the drill before fitting parts or changing bits and always remove the chuck key before switching it on.

Power leads to the machine should be kept short. If long, never allow them to trail on the floor, they should be slung from the ceiling.

Use both hands to guide and hold the drill and always wear goggles to avoid danger from splinters.

To avoid damaging the drill when drilling masonry, withdraw the tip every five seconds to stop it overheating. Or squirt water into the hole.

When drilling hard metal put a drop of turpentine or vinegar on the drill bit for lubrication.

When drilling thin or soft metal, place it between two pieces of wood. Drill through the wood and metal to stop rough edges or bent metal.

"I had six honest serving men - they taught me all I know,
their names were Where and What and When
and Why and How and Who."

Kipling

DRILLS

Place a strip of masking tape on the area of a metal or ceramic surface to be drilled. This will prevent the drill bit slipping.

Mark the depth of the hole required on the drill bit with a crayon, rubber band or masking tape. When the marker reaches the surface of the wood the hole will be the required depth.

A small drill bit can be straightened by placing it between two pieces of smooth hardwood and rolling it forward and backward with strong pressure on the top board.

To find the correct size of bit easily, measure the nail or screw with an adjustable spanner, then pick the bit that fits into the opening.

Most drill bit sets come in a storage case that can help you determine what size bit you need for each job. When drilling a hole for a nail, see which slot the nail fits into and choose the bit one size down. For a screw, choose the bit from the slot the screw fits into for the pilot hole.

To prevent shavings falling when drilling overhead, push the drill though a paper or clear plastic cup, open side upwards, and it will catch them.

When drilling blind holes in iron or steel, fine metal bits usually fall into the hole. To remove them, use a strong magnet and a soft iron or steel rod that is smaller in diameter than the hole. Push the rod to the bottom of the hole , press the magnet to the upper end. Keeping the magnet to the rod, pull it out of the hole and brush away the bits of metal. Repeat until all of the metal bits are removed.

If you have loose drill-bits, keep them in an old spectacle case to protect them. It is also handy for carrying bits in the pocket.

When drilling mirrors or sheet-glass, mark the spot with a felt tipped pen. Make a small well of putty and place it over the spot. Fill the indent with light oil. Drill slowly, using a carbide-tipped drill bit. The oil will keep the bit cool and aid the drilling process.

To prevent a tile cracking when inserting a screw in a drilled hole, make sure the rawl-plug is totally through the tile before screwing in the screw.

"They who practice what they preach
may have to put in some overtime."

ℱIXING
&
ℬONDING

No moving parts, no batteries.
No monthly payments and no fees.
Inflation proof, non-taxable, in fact it's quite reliable.
It can't be stolen, won't pollute.
One size fits all, do not dilute
It uses little energy but yields results enormously.
Relieves your tension and your stress,
invigorates your happiness.
Combats depression, makes you beam
and elevates your self esteem.
Your circulation it corrects
without complicated side effects.
It is, I think, the perfect drug.
May I prescribe, my friend, the hug!

TYPES OF NAILS

Round wire nails are sturdy general purpose nails with a large head.

Galvanised nails are used for exterior work. They are zinc-coated and will not rust in damp conditions. Galvanised clout nails have over-sized heads to hold roofing felt securely.

Oval wire nails are used when the nail has to be hidden, used generally for joinery.

Hardboard nails are used for carpentry, the head can be countersunk.

Masonry nails or round shank nails made from hardened steel are used when nails are inserted into brick or block walls or to fix timbers directly to a wall. Use extreme care when using these nails as they can easily snap. Always wear safety goggles and strike masonry nails square.

Rectangular section nails called cut floor brads have a spiral twist on the shank. They work like a screw and reduce the chance of loose squeaking boards. Blunt tips mean they are less likely to split the boards.

Panel pins are small nails easily inserted in wood. They are used for finer work like making up a picture frame. The small heads are sunk just below the surface with a nail punch and the hole covered with wood filler. Blunt the ends with a hammer to avoid thin pieces of wood splitting.

Tacks are used to secure carpets or upholstery.

To join a thin piece of wood to a thicker piece, the length of the nail should be at least twice the thickness of the thin piece of wood. If possible drive the nail through the thinner piece of wood into the thicker piece.

To make a strong nailed joint between pieces of timber or board, skew the nails as you hammer them in. Hold the joint steady with a nail hammered in the normal way. Angle the other nails at about 25 degrees, in pairs and facing each other. This will stop them pulling out easily. Always wear goggles when using a hammer.

If a small part or nail gets lost in grass or the workshop floor, put a nylon stocking over the end of a vacuum cleaner hose and turning on the cleaner play it over the area. The vacuum will suck it up and the nylon will hold it.

"The nail that sticks up gets pounded down."

NAILS

Nails provide a quick, strong method of joining wood which does not need to be taken apart. Use this type of fixing in areas where the finish is covered, such as floorboards.

Always use the correct nails or screws for the job in hand.

Dip large nails in paraffin or rub with soap to make them go in smoothly.

To prevent wood splitting, especially hardwoods like oak or maple or at the end of boards, pre-drill a hole slightly smaller than the nail thickness. Or insert a smaller nail first and then remove it before hammering in a larger one.

Blunt the point of a nail with a hammer before driving it into the wood. This will also prevent splitting.

Try not to run a line of nails along the same wood grain, otherwise the wood could split.

To hold a small nail in place without damaging fingers, use a hair comb or a V-notched piece of cardboard. If using a hand to hold the nail, keep the palm upwards.

Poor quality stainless steel nails can stain the surrounding wood.

When driving nails into a plaster wall, heat them first to make them go into more smoothly.

When driving cement-coated nails, always keep going all the way once started. Friction heats up the nail's coating and if stopped midway it cools down and tries to glue the nail in place.

If the head of a nail comes off while removing it, clamp the top of the nail with a pair of locking grip pliers. Use the claw hammer to pry against the pliers.

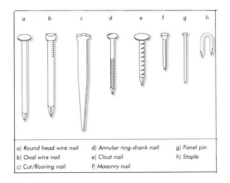

a) Round head wire nail   d) Annular ring-shank nail   g) Panel pin
b) Oval wire nail   e) Clout nail   h) Staple
c) Cut/flooring nail   f) Masonry nail

"You cannot hang everything on one nail."

Russian Proverb

TYPES OF SCREWS

Single-slot countersunk head screws are traditional screws with a long shank., used for hinges or joining pieces of wood.

Cross-head screws are probably the most popular type of screw because the cross-shaped slot tends to prevent the screwdriver slipping.

Round -head screws rest on top of the surface and are the easiest to remove. Used to fasten metal to wood, metal to metal or other material. They are threaded completely from point to head with sharp threads.

Mirror screws are most commonly used for fixing mirrors. They are a countersunk slotted screw, which is fixed first. A dome shaped chrome cover is then fastened into the top of the screw. When used for fixing mirrors or other fragile objects, a small rubber insert is set in the screw hole of the item to prevent the metal of the screw damaging it.

Chipboard screws are similar to the traditional countersunk type, but have a deeper thread allowing them to have a better grip in chipboard.

Twin thread screws have two deep threads interwoven with each other. The shank of the screws are narrower to give the screws greater grip.

Self-tapping screws are used in harder materials such as metal and fibreglass. A hole, the gauge of the shank, is drilled first. The screw then cuts a thread into the material as it is tightened.

Clutch head screws have a unique cross-head pattern which enables the screw to be done up , but not undone. It is used for fitting locks and other security devices. Before fitting, use an ordinary screw of the same size. This will enable minor adjustments to be made to the work before finally fitting the permanent clutch head screw.

Dry wall screws are thinner than a normal screw, with a sharper point. The thin head enables it to be driven into the surface of board or studwork easily.

Phillips screws have a cross-shaped slot and this lends itself to driving with a power bit.

"By the time a man realises that his father was right, he has a son who thinks he's wrong."

SCREWS

Screws give a strong, neat fixing to walls, man-made board, timber and even concrete, provided you choose the right fixing for the job.

Screws pull together the surfaces to be joined as the thread on the shank is rotated. The fixing is very strong and can be taken apart easily.

Choose brass or stainless steel plated screws for outdoor work. Black lacquered versions are available to match black hinges and latches.

A wood screw is described by two measurements - the length and diameter of the shank. The length is defined as the distance between the tip of the screw and the surface of the wood. The shank is given a gauge number with 6, 8 and 10 being the most commonly used. The higher the number the thicker the screw.

Rub screws with petroleum jelly before inserting them in wood, it makes them easier to remove when required.

When choosing a screw length, remember that the screw should penetrate two-thirds of the combined thickness of the materials being joined. The thicker the screw the greater the grip.

Brass screws can give an attractive finish, but the metal is soft and can be easily scratched or dented. The solution is to create a pilot hole, drive a regular steel screw of identical size into the hole. After the hole is created, remove the steel screw and replace it with a brass one.

Rub brass screws along a candle to lubricate them, making turning easier. Do not use too much force or the head will shear off.

Loosen a screw or nail by putting a drop of vinegar or lemon juice on the head and leaving it to soak overnight.

Tip the head of a painted over screw with a red-hot iron. This will remove the paint and expand the metal. When cool it should extract easily.

To remove a screw with a damaged slot another slot can be cut with a hacksaw blade if the head is exposed enough.

*"Ability is the power of applying knowledge
to practical purposes."*

SCREWS

To tighten a loose screw :-
Remove it and glue a piece of a wooden matchstick into the hole, reinsert the screw.

Insert one or two pieces of plastic cover electrical wire the length of the screw into the hole, then reinsert the screw.

Push a small piece of cotton material soaked with nail varnish into the hole before reinserting the screw.

Wind a few strands of steel wool or a small piece of aluminium foil around the screw.

If vibration causes nuts to constantly work loose, first add a lock washer, if it doesn't have one. Or, if there is room on the bolt, use two nuts, tightened toward each other so they lock solidly. Also try wrapping monofilament fishing line under the nut before tightening it on the bolt. Another possibility is to try wrapping the threads first with the teflon tape used in plumbing.

When fastening two pieces of wood together with screws, keep the pilot hole through the top piece slightly larger than the diameter of the shank of the screw. This will allow the wood screw to pull the two pieces of material tightly together. If the pilot hole is too small, the top piece can climb the threads of the screw and leave a gap between the two pieces.

Alternatively paint the inside of the hole with nail-varnish and re-screw. Or dip the screw in putty or glue before re-screwing.

To remove a tight rawlplug, insert a tight screw halfway into the plug, pull the screw and the plug out with pliers.

Rusty bolts can be freed by pouring cola over the bolt and leave until it dries or shake a few drops of Tabasco sauce over the bolt and leave for an hour.

Rusty screws and nails can be rejuvenated, by soaking them in neat vinegar overnight. Rinse and dry well in a low oven.

Screws and nails can be stored in recycled plastic or glass jars or in a multi drawer organiser. It is essential to label jars clearly or attach a sample screw/nail to the outside of the jar to see at a glance what is inside.

To store glass jars with metal lids, attach the lids to the underside of a shelf and screw the jars onto them.

"Necessity never made a good bargain."

GLUE

Polyvinyl glue is a white creamy glue usually sold in a plastic bottle with a nozzle. It is mainly used for craft or woodworking projects. It sets in an hour, dries clear and generally does not stain. It does not like damp conditions and should not be used outdoors.

Yellow carpenter's glue sets more quickly and is more resistant to water. It is not affected by varnish or paint, dries to a translucent finish and can be sanded.

Hot-melt glue is applied with a glue gun. It sets almost instantly on wood, metal, cloth, and ceramics. There are several formulas available to match to projects. Hot-melt glues do not adhere well to cold surfaces.

Extend the time it takes hot-melt glue to set by slightly pre-warming both the surfaces to be joined with a heat gun

Super glue or cyanocrylate is a liquid, adhesive, instant bonding glue. It bonds rapidly once pieces are joined, in less than 30 seconds. It is ideal for non-porous surfaces such as glass, certain plastics, ceramic, metal and can also be used to bond wood and paper. If it is accidentally dripped on skin, use nail polish remover to dissolve it. Instant bonding glue will dry inside the container very quickly so ensure the glue container's cap is replaced tightly, as soon as possible.

Super glue is expensive so it is generally only used for small repairs. The surfaces to be joined should be very clean and dry. Abrade lightly to provide a better grip.

Instant bonding or super glue will make an extra strong bond when mixed with bicarbonate of soda and can be used as a "filler" for small holes and indentations in almost any type of material. Place a few drops of the glue in the hole or indentation, while the glue is still wet add the soda, follow with a few more drops of glue. This will set and it will become very hard. This bonded area can be drilled. Remember a chemical reaction occurs immediately and creates a lot of heat for a short time.

Roughen smooth surfaces slightly before applying adhesives so they will grip more securely.

"Real security is based on wanting less - not having more."

GLUE

Glue caps have a tendency to get stuck after using the glue. To prevent this, dab a little petroleum jelly onto the cap before replacing and it will open easily the next time it's required.

Contact cements are used to bond veneers or to bond plastic laminates to wood for table-tops and counters. Coat both surfaces thinly and allow to dry before bonding. Since this adhesive does not pull apart, align the surfaces perfectly before pressing together. Use in a well-ventilated area.

Epoxy is the only adhesive with a strength greater than the material it bonds. It resists almost anything from water to solvents. Two-part epoxy adhesives (resin and hardener) are best where a strong repair is required on non-porous material such as metal, china and most plastics. It can be used in a warm temperature but read the manufacturer's instructions carefully, since drying times vary. The resin and hardener must be mixed thoroughly in the exact proportions to give a good bond.

To mix small amounts of epoxy glue use the metal cap of a spirit bottle, the plastic cap of a toiletry spray or make a small container from a piece of aluminium foil.

When working with epoxy glue there are two tubes, always put the correct cap back on each tube or they may not unscrew when next required.

With the exception of epoxy, excess adhesive will weaken the hold of the materials you are bonding. Apply a thin coat of glue, clamp securely, immediately wipe away any excess glue and allow to dry for the recommended amount of time.

PVA wood glues will bond wood (if it is clean and evenly surfaced) more strongly than screws or nails. It must be held in place securely until the glue sets. A glued joint will be very difficult to dismantle. PVA glue will not bond wood to plaster or mortar.

High strength adhesives are available that can bond most materials providing one of the surfaces is porous. Do not use this adhesive in permanently damp or wet areas.

Before re-gluing joints in wood warm the parts in the sun or over a heater or dip the parts in warm water and dry well. This will open the wood pores and allow the glue to easily soak into the wood.

"Consider the postage stamp;
Its usefulness consists in
the ability to stick to one thing till it gets there"

Josh Billings

When gluing a joint, a few strands of fine steel wool sprinkled on a glued surface before sticking together will result in a stronger bond.

Collect the sawdust after cutting wood and mix it with PVA glue to have a matching colour of wood filler.

When gluing veneer to a wood surface, use an old clothes iron to help. First use a sponge to wet the face of the veneer so that it won't curl. Next, apply a thin film of glue to both the surface and the underside of the veneer. Then, when the veneer is dry to the touch, use the clothes iron at a high setting to secure the veneer in place.

When positioning laminate for gluing, stick drawing pins all around the vertical edge of the surface to be covered. The heads of the pins should just be above the surface. The laminate can be positioned against them.

If laminate is stuck in the wrong position, put foil over it and iron until the plastic is warm enough to soften the glue, then move it into the correct position.

Most glue jobs require clamping, To stop the clamp bonding to the work, insert wax-paper between the clamp and the surface.

Old bicycle inner tubes cut into long, narrow strips make excellent clamps for repairing broken wooden furniture. After gluing a fractured joint, the rubber strips can be tightly stretched around the repair area to hold pieces in place while the glue is drying

Glue will soak more into the end grain of wood and can potentially result in starved glue joints. To help prevent this, "size" any end grain to be glued with a mixture of glue diluted with water. Dilute just enough that when it is applied, glue drops don't form at the lower edges of the wood.

Excess glue can be wiped off with a wet rag but this can push some of the glue into the wood pores. Another method is to leave the glue for about 15 minutes to form a thick skin and then use a sharp chisel or paint scraper to remove it.

When gluing joints together, run a strip of masking tape along the edges so that any excess glue will ooze onto the tape and be easily removed with the tape.

"Be thankful for problems. If they were less difficult,
someone with less ability might have your job."

GLUE

To stop movement while gluing timber, add shreds of steel wool, grains of sand or metal fillings (away from edges).

When wood-gluing work is less than successful, check the saw blades. If the blade in the saw is dull, it can loosen (but not remove) a layer of fibres on the edges to be joined. The glue may not be able to penetrate through this debris to solid wood, resulting in weak joints.

Pieces of wood being used outdoors can be glued together with an exterior oil based paint. Coat the surfaces to be joined and stick together as if using regular glue.

Warm vinegar will generally soften the most stubborn old glue on old furniture. Before re-gluing, dip the parts in warm water, and let them dry out completely to help open up the wood pores and allow the new glue to enter the wood more freely. Or warm the parts on top of a heater or in the sun.

Wood glue is generally water based. To unclog a nozzle, soak it in warm water. Cover the opening with tape while the nozzle is removed. When the glue in the nozzle is softened, remove it with a cocktail stick or toothpick.

Reseal a tube of glue with a screw in hook rather than replacing the cap. It is easier to remove when next required and the tube can be easily hung up to store.

To open a clogged tube of glue, dip a small drill bit into nail polish and bore into the hole. Clean the drill well after use.

Make a glue brush for water-based adhesive by threading a piece of cord through the barrel of an old ball-point pen. Fray the end of the cord and use as a brush. To refresh the 'brush', pull out some new cord and cut off the old.

Use wooden clothes pegs as mini clamps when gluing small items.

Most adhesive removers are solvent based and are highly flammable. Avoid using them near open flames and have adequate ventilation when using them. Damp mop the area with water and a small amount of detergent before using any sanding or electrical equipment. Or ensure that the solvent is thoroughly dry and the room ventilated for at least 24 hours.

"Glass, china and reputation.
Are easily cracked, but never well mended."

GLUE

Caulk and sealant are use to seal gaps in the interior or exterior of a house. They are available in colours or clear and many can be painted.

Caulk is glue-like and flexible, which are the characteristics necessary to seal a joint between dissimilar materials, or a joint that has movement.

The most popular formulation for weather-proofing applications is silicone acrylic, with excellent adhesion and a tight seal.

When applying caulks or sealant on wide gaps up to 1/2"(1.2cm) width/depth or larger areas, it is best to use a caulking gun. Caulk is also available in squeeze tubes for smaller jobs, such as around sinks and baths.

Use caulk for water leaks, energy loss through doors and window frames, gaps in siding and holes where concrete steps meet a wooden porch.

In a shower or bath enclosure, caulk is used to keep water from leaking up under or around the tiles at joints. Use between tile and the bath or shower tray, or on joints where walls meet

For a smooth clean finished appearance when applying caulk, choose the right caulk for the project - interior, exterior, mildew-resistant, paintable or tinted caulk.

Pre-clean the work area before removing any old caulk.

Remove any debris with a putty knife and any loose or flaking paint near the joint, by scraping or sanding.

Thoroughly clean, using a soap-and-water solution. Mildew can be eliminated, by adding a small amount of household bleach to the cleaning solution. Allow to dry completely. Silicon caulk will not adhere if there is any moisture on the surface.

Keep a roll of paper towels handy as well as a damp sponge. Use the towels to immediately remove any silicone caulk from hands as it is not water washable. The sponge is to moisten clean fingers for smoothing.

Cut the tip of the caulk tube with a sharp knife and screw on the nozzle.

"Some called open minds should be closed for repairs."

CAULK

Vary the width of the sealant bead by cutting the nozzle at different positions, the closer to the thread, the wider the bead will be. Check the width of the joint to be filled and cut the nozzle accordingly.

Mask around the work area so that excess caulk can be easily removed.

For best results, before starting, practise on a piece of scrap piece to get used to the application rate. Use a fluid, steady motion to lay the bead.

Rest the open end of the tube on the surface at the beginning of the crack. Trigger the gun as the nozzle is moved along the crack at the same speed as the caulk is being released. Do not 'stretch' the caulk along the joint.

As you approach the end of the joint, slowly release the pressure on the trigger.

Finish off by lightly smoothing the caulk with a slightly wet finger, damp rag, or a slightly wet spatula; this will ensure the best appearance. Be careful not to flatten out the bead.

The caulk bead should entirely fill the gap and be smooth enough to be virtually unnoticeable. Remove excess caulk with a razor blade.

When sealing or filling a corner, start from the corner and work outwards.

When sealing or filling large gaps, half-fill with thin strips of polystyrene before applying the sealant. This gives the sealant a solid base to bond on to.

All-acrylic and silicone-acrylic caulks are paintable; silicone caulk is not. Latex paint can be used after the caulk has dried for one hour, but four hours drying is required before painting with oil based paint.

If not using the whole tube of caulk, keep it fresh for next time by applying petroleum jelly to the inside of a wire connector and placing this over the tip or wrap the tip securely with insulating tape. When next using the caulk, squeeze out the dot of hardened caulk and the remainder should be still soft and pliable.

When finished using silicone from a tube, put it in a zip tight bag and it will stay fresh for months instead of days.

"System is not a card or filing case,
it is the right way of doing a thing."

Safety at Work

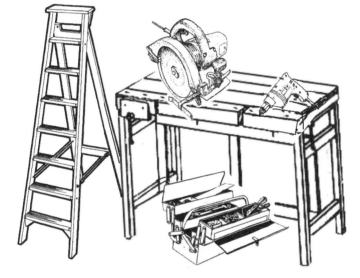

When things go wrong as they sometimes will
When the road you're trudging seems all uphill,
When the funds are low and the debts are high
And you want to smile but you have to sigh
When care is pressing you down a bit
Rest if you must, but don't you quit
Success is failure turned inside out
The silver tint on the clouds of doubt
And you can never tell how close you are
It may be near when it seems afar.
So, stick to the fight when you're hardest hit
It's when things go wrong that you mustn't quit.

In the Workshop

Workshop floors should be strong and level to support heavy equipment. The doorway should be wide enough to allow the entry and exit of bulky materials and projects in and out. The space should be dry, so tools won't rust. Provide enough electrical outlets, light, and ventilation for a safe and efficient workspace.

Any size of workshop should have, a smoke alarm, fire extinguisher, safety goggles, and first aid kit. All electrical outlets should be equipped with ground-fault circuit breakers. For emergencies, a telephone should be nearby.

Include in a first aid kit - regular and elastic bandages, antiseptic ointment, cotton swabs and balls, a tweezers, eye drops, elastic bandages with first-aid tape, gauze, a chemical cold pack, a first aid information handbook and a list of emergency phone numbers.

Use a tool belt to carry tools, either strapped to the waist or tied around the upper part of the ladder. Tools placed on top of stepladders out of view are dangerous.

Don't use a tool for anything other than its intended purpose. Using a wrench as a hammer may seem like a quick fix, but it may cause damage to the tool, the project, and possibly yourself. Remember, always use the right tool for the job.

Protective glasses or goggles should be worn when using power tools and when chiselling, sanding, scraping, or hammering overhead, especially if you wear contact lenses.

The proper face-mask should be worn when sanding or sawing or using substances with toxic fumes.

Wear ear protectors when using power tools, as some operate at noise levels that damage hearing.

Be careful of loose hair, clothing and jewellery, as they can get caught in tools.

Keep blades sharp as a dull blade requires excessive force, can slip, and cause accidents.

Always use the appropriate tool for the job and do not abuse tools.

" I like work. It fascinates me.
I can sit and look at it for hours."

Repair or discard tools with cracks in the wooden handles, or chips in the metal parts, that could fail and cause injury.

Make sure work is properly secured before drilling or sawing.

Unplug all power tools when changing settings or parts.

Keep any tool adjustment keys taped to the cord near the plug. This acts as a reminder to unplug the tool, as well as keeping the key safe.

Wear rubber-soled shoes when working with electric.

When using a power drill, choose a model that has a plastic non-conducting body. Unplug the drill before fitting parts and remove the chuck key before switching it on.

Watch cord placement so it does not interfere with the tool's operation.

Never use a power tool in wet or damp conditions, no matter how well grounded. Moisture readily conducts electricity.

Never tie back the blade guard of a circular saw or reach underneath it.

Before starting to cut, plane, or sand, thoroughly inspect the wood for metal objects such as nails or screws, especially if you are using power tools.

Read the owner's manual for all tools and know the proper use of each.

Use an old suitcase to store manuals safely and easily accessible.

Large plastic buckets are handy tool carriers. When not in use they can be hung up on the side of the workbench.

Keep all tools out of reach of children.

"Life is partly what we make it, and partly what it is made by the friends whom we choose."

LADDERS

When shopping for a ladder look for the proper ladder for the intended use, and buy the best quality ladder affordable. High-quality ladders are sturdier, safer, easier to use, and with proper care should last a lifetime.

Wooden ladders are the least expensive, they should be stored in a cool dry place.

Aluminium ladders are moderately priced. They are sturdy, lightweight and resistant to corrosion. They should not be used near electrical wiring as they can conduct electricity.

Fibreglass ladders are the strongest and most expensive. They are safer around electric wiring.

Roof ladders are made from softwood. Generally they have wheels fitted to slide up the roof and hooks to anchor the ladder over the ridge.

When working on fragile roofs, two ladders should be used side by side. A safety belt and rope should be fastened to a safe anchor.

Inspect a ladder before each use to make sure it is sound and firm. Any damages should be repaired and the ladder should be clean and dry.

On wooden ladders apply a coat of linseed oil or paint with clear wood preservative. These will not hide any defects that may develop.

An infrequently used, straight ladder can be checked by laying it flat on the ground and walking along each rung to test its strength.

Aluminium ladders are light and easily moved around. To prevent the rails at the bottom from becoming bent inwards, cut a piece of wood that fits exactly between the two rails. Wedge it into place at the very end of the ladder. Drill holes in the side rail and insert screws into the wood to prevent it falling out.

A ladder should be 3'(1m) above the highest level you need to stand at. Never stand above the third highest rung.

When placing a ladder up for use make sure that the foot of the ladder is one measure out for every four measures in height. This is especially important when using extension ladders.

"He who would climb the ladder must begin at the bottom."

Stepladders should be totally opened out to make sure that the cross braces are locked in position.

Never use a stepladder in the folded position leaning against something as the feet are angled wrong for it to be used this way and it will easily slip.

Never work from the top of a stepladder. A safe height is when the knees are below the top rung.

Always make sure that the ladder is level. Never set an extension ladder on sloping ground where both feet are not firmly on the ground. If necessary dig out the high area to level the ladder. Do not place loose objects like bits of wood or stones under the feet to level it.

Set up the ladder as close as possible to the work area and move the ladder when necessary. Do not overextend your reach as this can cause the ladder to slide or cause you to lose your balance

Ladders placed against poles or trees can be unstable. To eliminate this hazard, cover a length of strong chain with a rubber hose-pipe. Secure the chain to each side rail with bolts. This will allow the ladder to fit around the pole or tree and the rubber hose prevents it slipping.

When using a ladder outdoors, nail a piece of wood along one side of a board. Place the ladder on the board so that the piece of wood wedges it. This will stop the ladder slipping or sinking into soft ground.

"Stare up the steps - step up the stairs."

LADDERS

Another method to stop a ladder slipping on the ground is to drive strong spikes through the bottom of two old paint tin. Rest the bottom rails of the ladder in the tins. The spikes will anchor the ladder.

Never rest ladders on guttering or a window-sill.

Glue strips of car mats to the rungs of a wooden ladder for improved grip. Wear soft, rubber soled shoes that have a good grip.

When using a ladder indoors, put an old pair of thick socks on the bottom of the rails to prevent it slipping. Or fill canvas bags with sand and set the ladder in these, secure the bags to the rails with wire.

To make working on a ladder easier, use elastic cords to secure a small plastic basket to the top of a stepladder to hold tools. On an extension ladder, slide a broom handle through a hollow rung and hang a bucket for tools from that. Keeping tools close at hand will save several trips up and down the ladder.

To stop a ladder hanging on a wall from being easily knocked down, attach an old leather belt to the wall halfway along the ladder. Buckle the belt around the ladder and it will stay securely against the wall.

To hang up a stepladder securely, insert a closed eye-screw into the wall at the top height of the ladder. Twist the hook of a wire coat hanger around the screw. Slip the horizontal wire of the hanger over the top step to hold the ladder against the wall.

When moving a ladder, use the right technique to avoid injury. The correct way to handle a ladder is to hold it upright against your body. With one hand, hold a rung about thigh level. Use your other hand to hold a rung about head high and on the opposite side of the lower rung. Set the ladder about 2'(1m) from where you want it and slowly lower it to position.

Do not balance heavy or pointed objects on the steps of a ladder or near hatches in a loft as they can easily fall and hurt anyone standing below them.

If your means suit not with your ends,
pursue those ends which suit with your means."

FIXTURES & FITTINGS

"The secret to happiness and well-being is no mystery.
All it takes is the ability to do the following:
Forget. Apologise.
Admit errors. Avoid mistakes.
Listen to advice. Keep your temper.
Shoulder the blame.
Make the best of things.
Maintain high standards.
Think first and act accordingly.
Put the needs of others before your own.
Forgive."

HELPFUL HINTS

To stop birds from eating freshly set window putty, mix some black pepper into it.

When cupboards are damp, fill a plastic-lidded tin with charcoal briquettes, punch holes in the lid and place in cupboard, or tie a few sticks of chalk together and place them in the back of the cupboard.

For musty smells, place a small tin of cat litter deodoriser in the bottom of the cupboard.

To fix a chair or table that wobbles, find a button that is the right thickness and hot glue it to the short leg. The chair or table will sit straight. Or put a blob of putty on the uneven leg, shape to the diameter of the leg , when dry paint or stain to match.

If one table leg is shorter than the rest, get some glue and pieces of newspaper and keep applying until the leg stops wobbling. When it's at the correct height, stain or paint the paper to match the rest of the legs.

Secure a loose chair leg by wrapping the loose end with small strip of nylon or elasticised stocking, apply glue to both the leg and the stocking before re-inserting.

If the seats on a wicker chair are loosening, mix equal parts of white vinegar and water. Dampen the wicker that is loose with the solution and place in the sun. The wicker will shrink and tighten.

When filling a hole with wood putty, insert staples into the bottom of the hole, keep them below the surface. This will give the putty something to adhere to for a stronger bond.

When finishing a piece of wood, remove any pencil marks with an eraser before sanding.

A good polish mixture is - 1/2 cup each of boiled linseed oil, turpentine and vinegar. Mix together and shake well. Apply with a soft cloth and wipe dry. Wipe again with another soft cloth.

For a polish for wood, combine 1gall(5ltr) hot water, 4tbsp olive oil and 4tbsp cider vinegar. Dip a soft cloth in the mixture, wring the cloth almost dry Apply to dry wooden, furniture and wipe with a clean soft rag. The mixture adds oil to the wood and will hide small scratches and scuffs without damaging the wood.

"The fastest way to find something lost is to replace it."

DOORS

External flush doors are of heavier construction than internal doors. They are usually faced with water-resistant plywood. The core is made of narrow battens forming a lattice and solid blocks are built into the lattice to receive locks and other door furniture.

Internal doors are faced with hardboard and have a lighter core of hardwood slats, wood slats or softwood spirals.

When purchasing a new door measure the dimensions of the door-frame rather than the old door. The height is measured from the floor level to the rebate in the head of the frame. The width is measured between the rebates in the jambs. The thickness of the door is the same as the width of the rebate.

Sticking or hard to close doors can be caused by a number of problems. First check the hinges to see if they remain firmly in place when the door is moved. If they are loose then tighten each screw on the hinge.

If a screw will not tighten, try inserting a longer screw of the same diameter. Or insert a piece of a matchstick into the hole and then the original screw again.

If a door is sticking on the hinge side the cause can be excess paint on the edge of the door. Strip off the paint and repaint with one coat.

When door hinges are not properly fitted the door will not close properly. Remove the offending hinge and pare off more wood from the recess.

If too much wood is pared off put a piece of cardboard under the hinge.

Another reason for a door sticking is that the door may be off square. Check the door and frame for areas of paint rubbed off. Or close the door and push a thin piece of card between it and the frame. Move the card around the door and where it will not pass easily is where the problem is.

Try rubbing the area with polish or candle wax but if this doesn't work then it will be necessary to plane off some of the wood.

Doors scraping on the floor can have a piece of abrasive paper put underneath the area and the door pulled forward and backward on the paper. Keep putting sheets of cardboard underneath the sandpaper to raise it and keep the pressure on.

"Don't ever slam a door, you might want to go back in."

DOORS

The problem with a rattling door is usually at the hinge. Loop a rubber band around the hinge pin and secure with a knot. Let the remainder of the band hang down between the hinge. When the door is closed the rubber band will stop the door rattling.

It can be dangerous when there are young children in the house and doors swing closed freely. To make them close more slowly, take out the pin from the top hinge and wrap a strip of self-adhesive tape around it then reinsert the pin.

Doors that are taken down frequently should have a little notch removed at the point of the hinge where the head of the hinge pin sits. This will make it easier to insert the point of a screwdriver to remove the pin.

On patio doors rub the tracks with a candle to keep them moving freely.

To keep patio doors securely closed, cut a piece of pipe the length of the track where the door slides open. Put the pipe in the track when the doors are closed.

Apply spray starch to doors and to painted walls along hallways and stairways where fingerprints accumulate. The coating will resist marks better.

To loosen a sticking lock, put a little powdered graphite or rub a pencil lead on the key and work it into the lock.

If there is difficulty in closing the latch of a door it may be that the door or frame has moved causing the strike and the strike plate to be out of line.

The easiest way to fix the problem is to make the plate aperture larger by filing it. To ascertain how much to file off, apply lipstick to the bolt and close the door. The bolt will leave a lipstick mark on the plate and this can be used as a filing guide.

Sometimes a small amount of timber may have to be chiselled from behind the plate to allow the bolt to operate.

When installing a new or replacement lock, position the keyhole so that the cuts of the key will be inserted upwards. This will reduce dirt, dust, and water settling in the lock mechanism, making it stiff to operate.

"Efficiency means accomplishing more with less exertion and less expense."

WINDOWS

When dealing with broken glass, handle with care. Wear a pair of thick protective gloves, a pair of goggles and strong shoes.

To re-glaze a broken windowpane, first, remove any jagged edges of glass with a pair of pincers. If the glass is only cracked, put adhesive tape over the cracks and use a glass cutter to cut around the pane 1"(2.5cm) from the frame. Put a piece of cloth over the glass and tap it gently from the inside to separate one piece at the time and remove it.

Remove the old putty with a putty knife or a wood chisel and hammer. Pull out any old glazing pins and sand the frame down with glass-paper. Apply a coat of primer and allow to dry. Protect the window with a sheet of strong plastic or hardboard.

Apply paraffin oil to putty that is difficult to remove, it dissolves the linseed oil in the putty, making it crumble and easier to remove.

Another way is to brush the putty with hydrochloric acid and leave for a few minutes, the putty will soften and remove easily.

Heat helps to loosen putty, wrap the end of a soldering gun with aluminium foil, heat the tool and run it across the putty. The foil prevents the putty from ruining the tip and allows the heat to penetrate the putty.

Measure the height and width of the opening then deduct 1/8"(3mm) from each measurement. The glass should fit easily into the frame. Check the dimensions in a few places to make sure the widow frame is square.

Order the glass, putty and pins to suit the frame to be glazed. Slit two short pieces of garden hose and use to grip the sheet of glass when carrying it.

Before cutting a pane of glass, make a pattern on a piece of paper to the exact measurements. Place the paper under the sheet of glass and it will be easier to cut.

To prevent a straight edge from slipping when cutting glass, use a metal one and rub a dry bar of soap along the cutting line on the glass and also the underside of the straight edge.

"Wisdom isn't the acquisition of knowledge. It's knowing which knowledge is worth acquiring."

Frank Tyger

WINDOWS

If using a wooden ruler or straight edge, wet the underside of the ruler before placing it on the glass.

Before running the glass cutter on the glass, run an artist's brush dipped in turpentine along the cutting line to prevent chipping.

Glazier's pliers are very useful for breaking off cut glass. Since these would be used infrequently make a temporary pair when required by taking a regular door hinge, the gap between the hinge flanges is about the same thickness as a sheet of glass. Put a strip of masking tape on the inside of each flange. Place the hinge around the glass and grip the hinge with a pair of pliers.

Work the putty in the palms of the hand until it is pliable. If it feels oily work it back into the putty and remove any excess by squeezing it in newspaper.

Old, dry putty can be rejuvenated by making a dent in a ball of putty, adding a dash of linseed oil and kneading it in thoroughly.

To soften hardened putty, put it into a strong plastic bag and place in hot water for a short time.

An easy way to knead putty is to put it inside a plastic bag and knead in the bag. Dust the hands with flour when using putty and it will stop it sticking to them.

Roll the putty into 6"-9"(15-22cm) rolls about 3/4"(2cm) in diameter. Squeeze the putty rolls into the rebate in the frame with the thumb and forefinger, making a continuous strip all around the frame.

Place the glass in position and press gently into place all around the edges. Do not apply pressure to the centre of the pane. Any excess putty will ooze out giving a good seal.

Secure the glass in position by tapping in two glazing pins into the wooden frame, on each side of the glass. Place a sheet of thin cardboard against the glass and using a small hammer, holding it sideways on the glass, and with a sliding action, drive in the pins.

When mending glass in a metal frame use the proper glazing clips to secure the glass.

"Work is the best thing ever invented for killing time."

Take more rolls of putty and starting at the top spread the putty along the edge of the glass with a putty knife. Continue with the two sides and then the bottom of the window. When doing the final levelling off dip the knife in water to give a smooth finish.

Keep the putty knife clean by cutting a slit in the side of a tin can, make the slit the thickness of the putty knife blade. To clean off the blade, insert it in the slit and pull it straight out. The putty in the tin can be re-used.

Putty knives can be cleaned with steel wool dipped in linseed oil.

Trim off any excess putty on the inside of the window and remove any finger marks from the glass with cotton wool dipped in methylated spirit.

The putty should be allowed to harden for 7-14 days before painting. Do not leave for longer or the putty will dry out and crack.

Store unused putty wrapped up in foil and in a tub so that it lasts longer.

"Learning is finding out what you already know.
Doing is demonstrating that you know it.
Teaching is reminding others that they know it
just as well as you.
You are all learners, doers, teachers."

Richard Bach

Gutters & Windows

Before cleaning gutters, place a basin under the down pipe to prevent debris from blocking the drains.

Wearing a strong pair of gloves, remove leaves, twigs, and other debris from gutter troughs. Cut a piece of wood to a slightly smaller curve than the gutter and use this to scrape the inside. Brush with a stiff brush and hose all debris out of the system.

Rather than having to keep moving the ladder when removing debris from a gutter, attach a tin can, the correct size to fit the gutter, to a long pole and pull this along the gutter. It will remove most of the debris.

Clean a blocked downspout by spraying with a garden hose turned on full force. If the spouting is blocked push a piece of heavy electric waste cable down into it while flushing out with a hose.

Add mesh screens to deflect leaves, twigs, and other debris over the edge of the gutter. A leaf strainer will admit water and filter out debris.

Check the joints and seal any leaky ones by applying silicone sealant or caulking around the seams between sections on the inside and outside of the gutter.

To repair a small hole, use a putty knife to patch on a thin coat of roofing cement, extending the cement beyond the hole in all directions.

For holes larger than 1/2"(1.2cm), cover with roofing cement and embed a sheet metal patch in the cement. Apply another coat of cement over the patch.

Spray-on car undercoating is good for sealing joined sections of guttering. For patching put a piece of wire gauze over the hole and spray on the paint

Short runs of guttering should be fitted level. Water will always find the trap without tilting.

"People who say it cannot be done
should not interrupt those who are doing it."

THE
BUILDERS
YARD

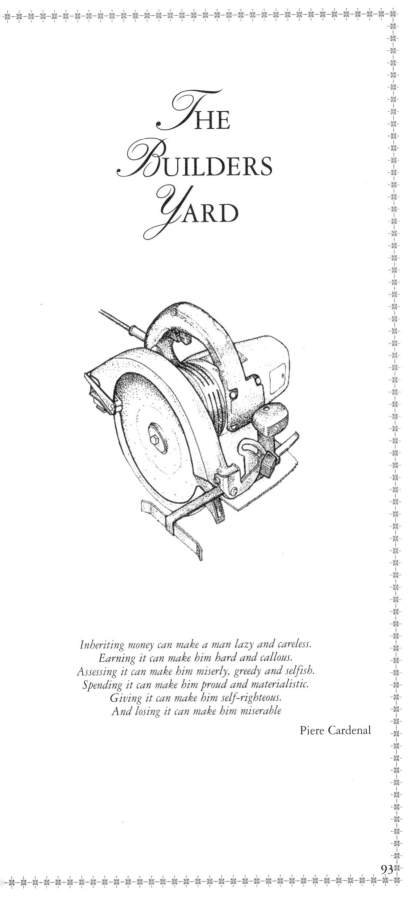

Inheriting money can make a man lazy and careless.
Earning it can make him hard and callous.
Assessing it can make him miserly, greedy and selfish.
Spending it can make him proud and materialistic.
Giving it can make him self-righteous.
And losing it can make him miserable

Piere Cardenal

WOOD

Hardwoods include Ash, Beech, Cherry, Chestnut, Elm, English Oak, Imported Oak, Japanese Oak, Lime, Mahogany, Rosewood, Teak and Walnut.

Hardwood is strong and durable and more expensive than softwood because of its longer life span. It is often used for furniture making.

The timber should be seasoned and stored correctly. Seasoning helps to strengthen the wood. If it has not been covered during storage it can be permanently damaged by watermarks. Check the quality of the wood purchased for suitability for any particular work.

The most common, traditional hardwood flooring is mosaic block flooring in panels. These panels are flexible and easy to lay. There is a low risk of allergy because it is a natural product and easy to clean. Modern hardwood flooring comes in a wide range of timbers.

Softwoods include Cedar, Deal, Hemlock, Larch, Pine, Spruce, Redwood, Whitewood and Yew.

Softwoods are cheaper than hardwood but they will deteriorate faster, especially if used for external projects. They need to be treated with wood preservers or paints to protect the wood from the elements.

Many softwoods have a high resin content giving a build up of a seeping sticky liquid in pockets on the surface. These sections and any knots must be treated with knotting before priming to seal the surface, or they will spoil the overall finish of the timber.

A common problem with softwood is that it can be split in places or warped. Always check the quality of the wood purchased for suitability for the job in hand.

Softwood used in a loft space, for rafters or joists, should be treated with a preservative for woodworm and/or rot.

Exposed floorboards should be treated with a clear, lacquer finish to stop grime working its way into the surface. This will also enhance the appearance by showing the natural colour of the wood.

"You cannot carve rotten wood"

Sawn timber comes direct from being cut into sections and appears rough. Planed timber comes machine cut and smooth edged.

Block-board is usually made from rectangular strips of softwood glued and bonded together under high pressure. These strips are then sandwiched between a wood veneer, such as birch. A single veneer on both sides is known as 3-ply. A double veneer on both sides is called 5-ply.

Block-board is only suitable for interior work, as the glues used in its construction are not waterproof.

If the surface requires painting then both sides should be covered in order to equalise the surface tensions and aid the shaping of the block board.

Chipboard is made from resin coated particles of softwood. The particles are evenly spread over a flat plate and heat bonded together under high pressure.

Other types of chipboard available are flooring grade, melamine veneered (Formica worktops), plastic veneered, white or coloured melamine (used in making furniture) and wood veneered.

Chipboard is an economical material and suitable for many internal jobs, if well supported. There are waterproof grades available for using in damp conditions.

Hardboard is a versatile product made by the high pressure forcing of softwood pulp into sheets. The standard hardboard sheet is finished on one side and a textured underside.

Other types of hardboard available are duo faced, medium, oil-tempered, painted, perforated (commonly known as pegboard) and plastic faced.

MDF (Medium Density Fibreboard) is produced, by bonding wooden fibres together under high pressure. The manufacturing method used ensures that it has a fine texture throughout.

MDF is an extremely versatile product suitable for many interior projects such as shelving, cupboards etc. It cannot be used for outside work exposed to wet conditions.

Due to the fineness of the fibres, it is advisable to use a mask when sawing the boards to avoid inhaling the fine dust particles.

"Want of care does more damage than want of knowledge."

WOOD

Sheets of plywood are produced by bonding constructional veneers together face to face, ensuring that the grains run in alternative directions. Sheets are bonded on both sides of the original piece to keep the tensions equal. The basic number required is therefore three sheets, which is known as 3-ply. By adding sheets equally to both sides, a stronger ply is produced. Ply thickness is always in odd numbers. This procedure helps to reduce warping

Plywood is available in standard, plastic faced and wood faced. There is a more expensive plywood for external use. The adhesives used in its construction are waterproof.

Plywood can be used for many jobs in the same way as solid wood. It is stronger but more expensive than chipboard, and often has a more attractive surface, which can be either varnished or painted.

All the above wood sheets or boards are available in a variety of thickness. They should all be stored flat to avoid twisting or warping and care should be taken to ensure that the sides and corners are protected.

When storing wood flooring and panelling, stack the boards on stickers to allow air space between rows and help reduce shrinkage of wood joints.

Any timber intended for internal use may shrink. The warm conditions can lead to minor changes. To ensure correct measurements, store the timber in the environment for 5-7 days prior to cutting giving it a chance to acclimatise

Long strips or battens of wood are prone to warping in storage. Check that purchases are straight.

When ordering wood from a timber yard, remember that if you give the wood measurements required but ask for it to be planed, then the finished measurements will be smaller.

Use chalk to make notes on boards instead of pencil and the surface will not be marred.

If using filler on wood add a little instant coffee powder to make the colour a better match.

To avoid chipping when cutting laminate always score the cutting line with a very sharp blade and cut it right side upwards with a fine-toothed tenon saw.

"A wedge from itself splits the oak tree "

For a project to turn out as strong, solid, and lasting as if a professional woodworker built it, check with a square after each cross cut. Edges on boards that will be edge-joined must be absolutely square, so carefully check all sides. If a cut is not exactly square, use a block plane to trim.

Stairs creak because wood is rubbing on wood. Either a tread or riser is not secure. If the under-side of the staircase is accessible, under each stair, the end of the treads are often supported by wedges. Locate the creaking stair by having someone walk on the stairs and tighten the offending one by tapping the wedge ends with a hammer.

There should be tongued and grooved joints between the rise and tread sections of each step. Sometimes there are glued triangular blocks in place that may need tightening, or replacing with metal repair plates or use shelf brackets.

Jointed treads and risers can be drilled and clearance holes countersunk approximately 10"(25cm) apart through the tread. At the top of the riser drill pilot holes in the same positions. Insert screws into the front of the tread to the riser. Tighten the screws and cover the heads with filler to match the varnish. Sand the area for a smooth finish.

Stop squeaky floorboards or creaking stairs by locating the two boards that are causing the problem. Squirt some all-purpose glue into the crack, wipe away any excess glue and leave to dry. Or shake talcum powder or French chalk between the boards.

Gaps between floorboards can be filled with a quantity of wallpaper glue mixed to a very thick paste and shredded brown paper added. Leave slightly proud and sand when fully dry. Stain and seal with the rest of the floor.

"As you slide down the banister of life, may the splinters never point in the wrong direction!"

Irish Blessing

MARBLE

Occasionally wash marble surfaces with tepid water and wipe dry with a clean cloth. Wipe surface with a damp chamois to stop streaking. Or wash with a solution of hand dishwashing detergent and warm water, rinse and wipe dry.

A light coat of colourless wax can protect the surface of marble but is not essential. Do not use wax on a white marble surface, as it can tend to yellow it. A marble sealer can be applied to clean marble. This will protect from staining and allow grime to be wiped off with a damp cloth.

Acid fruit juices, carbonated beverages or other acids will remove the shiny surface of marble if allowed to remain on it for any length of time. Wipe up acid spills immediately, and wipe surface with a wet cloth. If the surface is etched, polishing may be required.

To remove oily stains like butter, hand cream or lotion from marble, immediately spread an absorbent fine powder such as cornstarch on the surface. Brush off after a few minutes and reapply more powder. Leave for 24 hours. Scrub with hot, sudsy, detergent solution and stiff brush. Or wipe with ammonia-dampened cloth. Rinse and wipe dry.

If these alkaline solutions don't remove all the oil, you can try a solvent. Make a poultice dampened with acetone or amyl acetate or with home dry cleaning fluid. Make sure there is good ventilation by opening windows to let the fumes escape. Do not use near spark or flame, and only leave on the surface for a short time.

If marble is stained with tea, coffee, colours bleached from paper or soft drinks. Make a poultice from white absorbent material such as a napkin, blotter or paper towel dampened with 20% peroxide, hair bleaching strength, and a few drops of ammonia. Or make a paste with the peroxide, ammonia and whiting. The poultice should be left on the stain from 1 hour up to 48 hours, depending on the age and depth of the stain. Plastic wrap, held in place by masking tape, can be put over the poultice to keep it damp; otherwise it will have to be re-dampened with the chemical periodically. Mix only enough poultice for immediate use, mix a second batch later if another application is required..

Rust stains on marble are usually the result of metal items such as a lamp, or a decorative plant metal container. Use a commercial rust stain remover. Follow directions exactly and only leave on the surface for a short time as the acid in many rust removers can etch the surface.

" Idleness is the rust of the mind."

TILES

When laying new floor tiles save time before applying the mortar or adhesive by first dry fitting the tiles on the area to be tiled. Mark any tiles needing to be cut. This will help determine how to get the best design and fit, and avoid the mess of pulling up tiles after the mortar is applied.

When working with ceramic tiles always wear safety goggles and thick work gloves.

Tiles are cut by scoring the glazed surface with a glass cutter, then snapping off the surplus.

Always make sure to work squarely. Before commencing tiling, draw a horizontal line with a spirit level or a vertical line with a plumb line.

Use a spreader with saw-like edges to spread adhesive to an even thickness. The ridges left in the adhesive will help to bed down the tiles.

To replace a broken tile, place masking tape in two strips diagonally to form an X shape on the tile, this will help stop the drill bit slipping.

Using a 5mm bit, drill holes at intervals along each strip of masking tape. Only drill the depth of the tile, wrap a piece of masking tape around the drill bit at the required depth to use as a guide.

Remove all the old grout from around the tile, ensuring not to damage the surrounding tiles.

Using a cold chisel and hammer chip at the tile, starting from the middle and working out to the edges along the masking tape.

Remove the masking tape, taking away most of the broken tile with the tape. Use an old wood chisel bevel side down to remove any remaining bits of tile and grout, taking care not to damage the surrounding tiles.

Carefully remove the old tile adhesive from the wall, leaving a clean flat surface to apply new adhesive

Place the new tile into the space to see if it fits and to make sure it is even, if the tile rocks then the surface is not even. This also gives a guide as to the amount of tile adhesive to be applied.

"Spare no expense to make everything as economical as possible."

TILES

Apply the adhesive to the back of the tile using the adhesive spreader, use sparingly as the tile has to sit flush.

Carefully put the tile into place, making sure all sides and corners are flush with the surrounding tiles. Clean off any adhesive on the face of the tile and the surrounding areas.

Use tile spacers to get an even spacing around the tile and leave for 24 hours or as recommended on the tile adhesive instructions.

Once the tile is securely fixed in position remove the tile spacers and grout around the tile. Use a plastic grout-finishing tool to give the grout a smooth finish. When the grout has dried, polish off with a dry cloth.

Tiles can be put on most materials providing the surface is firm and flat.

Use a masonry drill to make holes for screws. Always use plugs in the wall when inserting screws. Preferably screws should be inserted between tiles to avoid cracking the glaze.

On a ceramic tile counter top protect against chipping by using a cutting board. Protect against scratches, especially on glazed tiles, by using a heat-proof mat under hot pans and electrical appliances on the counter. Avoid hard blows to avoid chipping tiles.

Wash with detergent solution, and rinse. To clean dingy grout, occasionally apply a solution of chlorine bleach and water, leave for 5 minutes; rinse thoroughly and wipe dry. General-purpose household cleaners may be used if the label states they can be used on ceramic tile; follow directions exactly. NEVER use scouring powders or other abrasives, they will scratch the finish. Creamy liquid appliance wax can be used to protect tiles and grout.

To find out how many tiles are required, first measure the area to be tiled, then using the chart calculate how many tiles you need. Take into account any tiles needing cut to fit the wall, by adding 10%

Area in Sq Metres	1	2	3	4	5	6	7	8
Tile Size			Number of Tiles Required					
100x100mm (4"x4")	100	200	300	400	500	600	700	800
152x152mm (6"x6")	43	86	129	172	215	258	301	344
200x152mm (8"x6")	33	66	99	132	165	198	231	264
200x200mm (8"x8")	25	50	75	100	125	150	175	200
250x200mm (10"x8")	20	40	60	80	100	120	140	160

"Always investigate before you speculate."

CONCRETE

Numerous outside repairs are fixed with concrete or mortar. The main constituent of concrete and mortar is cement. This is purchased as a fine powder made from a lime and clay mixture that sets hard when mixed with water.

Cement hardens and deteriorates if kept for a long time after the bag is opened. For this reason it may be more economical only to purchase the amount required for the work in hand.

If cement has to be stored, keep it covered and away from walls and floors. Outdoors cement should be stored off the ground and covered with polythene or tarpaulin.

Ordinary cement is grey in colour, but white cement is available, but more expensive.

Concrete is composed of cement, sand, gravel and water. Mortar consists of cement sand and water. Sand is called fine aggregate while gravel is coarse aggregate.

Aggregate can be purchased ready mixed or the sand and gravel purchased separately.

Use clean sharp sand or concrete sand for concrete and clean soft sand or builder's sand for mortar.

The proportion of aggregate to cement varies according to the requirements of the work in hand. The aggregate used for building foundations would be very coarse while fine graded builders sand would be used to make mortar to fill a crack.

When laying concrete always allow time to do the job properly. However once the concrete is mixed the work should be completed within two hours, discard any remaining after this time. If concrete dries too quickly it may eventually cause cracks.

Measure all the ingredients, including the water to obtain uniform concrete when mixing different batches.and to avoid waste.

To mix concrete, put the required amount of aggregate in a broad pile on a clean flat hard surface like a sheet of plywood. Shake the measured cement on top. Using a spade or a shovel, mix the aggregate from the bottom with the cement until the whole pile is an even colour.

*"Three o'clock is always too late or too early
for anything you want to do."*

CONCRETE

Make a hollow in the top and pour in a little clean water, mixing from the edge to the centre. Add more water and continue to mix, turning in dry material until the whole mixture is wet. The amount of water should be kept to a minimum, as too much gives a weaker result.

Flatten the heap and cut into it with the spade. The ridges formed should stay there. If they flow back into a smoother surface, the mixture is too wet. It is important to get the correct consistency, if the concrete is too dry it will not make a strong bond with masonry.

Lay polythene sheeting over fresh concrete and weigh down with a scattering of sand to allow for slow drying. Full drying and setting will take from four to ten days, according to atmospheric conditions.

Wash down all boards and tools immediately ensuring that sand or concrete does not get into house or yard drains.

Thin sections of concrete do not wear well.

A small diamond shaped pointing trowel is most useful for carrying out repairs in concrete.

When repairing simple cracks, mix a small amount of PVA adhesive with the sand and cement mix and insert into the crack, leave to dry.

If the edges of the crack are worn away , use a cold chisel to cut off the old concrete, making a recess with clean edges. Remove all loose material with a pointed trowel and a stiff brush. Make a mixture of 1 part cement to 3 parts sharp sand. Brush the crack with water and using the point of a trowel force the concrete well into the crack, pressing down thoroughly. When full level off.

When laying concrete to extend a path, surround the boundary with pieces of wood to restrict the concrete. Leave in place until the concrete is set.

Level the surface with straight edged board moved up and down over the area.

A flat piece of wood or metal with a handle called a float, can be moved backwards and forwards over the concrete to give a smoother surface.

To extend the working time with plaster, add 1/4tsp vinegar per 1pt(450ml) of plaster or purchase a proprietary retarder.

"Every job is a self-portrait of the person who did it."

BRICK & STONE

Bricks are made from clay and other materials, formed into shapes, then fired in a kiln making them strong and durable. Red brick contains large amounts of iron; yellow brick contains little iron.

Remove dust from interior bricks with a vacuum cleaner. Freshen periodically with commercial brick cleaner.

Brick may be purchased sealed or unsealed. Sealed brick is easier to keep clean. Vacuum regularly and wipe with a damp cloth to remove dirt. Clean very dirty brick with a mild detergent solution, rinse well, and wipe dry.

To seal a brick floor, first scrub the surface using a brush or sponge and detergent, rinse with clear water. Make sure any dirty wash water is completely removed from crevices. Allow floor to dry thoroughly. Using a recommended sealer, paint the brick. Let it dry and apply a second coat. To keep a good seal on the brick apply a new coat of sealer once a year.

Mix 1oz(25g) soap and 1oz(25g) table salt with enough water to make a cream. Rub mixture into brick surface with cloth, allow to dry for 10-15 minutes and remove with a stiff brush.

To remove soot from brick or stone, dissolve 4oz(100g) laundry soap in boiling water. When the mixture has cooled, add 8oz(200g) powdered pumice and 4fl oz(100ml) household ammonia. Mix thoroughly. Use a stiff brush to remove as much soot as possible. Paint the surface with the soap mixture, leave on for 30 minutes, remove with a stiff brush and warm water. Rinse thoroughly with warm water.

Stone or brick fireplaces can be cleaned more easily if a penetrating sealer containing tung oil, is applied. This is moisture resistant and forms a tough coating which can be washed with soap and water

Rub dry slate with a soft cloth dipped in lemon oil furniture polish. Using a fresh cloth, wipe off excess oil and buff the stone. This makes stone uniformly dark and glossy. Do not use wax on fireplaces as it is affected by heat.

"You cannot build a reputation on things you are going to do."

CAST & WROUGHT IRON

Cast iron is heavy, hard, and brittle. It may break if dropped. Cast iron will rust if it is not seasoned. Keep and store in dry conditions to avoid rust. Put paper towels in items stored for long periods, to absorb moisture. Do not put lids on pans when storing as this may increase moisture build-up.

Cast iron items not pre-treated should be well seasoned before using for the first time. Brush unsalted fat on surfaces. Heat until grids begin to smoke, wipe off extra fat, wash in soapy water and dry thoroughly immediately. Wipe with a thin coating of fat or oil. If not properly seasoned, cast iron pans will drip dark liquid into food.

After using cast iron utensils for baking, brush surfaces with a soft plastic brush or wipe gently with a paper towel while still warm, to remove crumbs.

Do not wash metal grids or put any water on them. The seasoned surfaces darken and prevent sticking. If grids without a non-stick finish begin to stick, or are stained by foods being spilled on them, wash grids with warm suds, rinse, wipe dry, and re-season with unsalted fat.

Stubborn burned-on food or grease is best removed by soaking in hot water. Use a plastic scouring pad if necessary. Soak in a solution of 3tbsp of washing soda or bicarbonate of soda per 2pt(1 2ltr) of water to remove burned on food or grease. Do not scour off the seasoned finish build up acquired over long use or the utensil will have to be re-seasoned.

Rust may be scoured with fine steel wool or scouring powder but re-seasoning of the utensil will be necessary.

Wrought iron used for decorative items is generally made from the purest form of iron so it is generally more resistant to rust than cast iron.

A protective coat of liquid wax will make cleaning easier and retard rusting. Do not use liquid wax on fireplace accessories, as it is flammable. When cleaning is required, wash with a damp cloth and wipe dry.

To remove rust stains, rub with kerosene, and scour with fine grade steel wool. If rust is difficult to remove, allow kerosene to remain long enough to loosen. Commercial rust removers may also be used.

"The slogan that leads to success - Adopt, Adapt, Improve."

Stainless Steel & Chrome

Stainless steel is an alloy of iron containing more than 10% chromium. Stainless steel resists stains but occasionally dulls or shows oily marks. This steel is noted for its hardness and is used for utensils, tableware, sinks, counter tops, and small appliances. In the process of making it, a little of the chromium in the alloy is used to form the hard oxide coating on the surface. If this is removed through corrosion or wear, the steel rusts like regular steel.

Rub stainless steel sinks with olive oil to remove streaks.

Remove rust stains from stainless steel with lighter fuel. When removed wipe with regular kitchen cleaner.

A cloth dampened with rubbing alcohol will remove water spots from stainless steel. Use club soda to give a shine to stainless steel.

For a good shine on bathroom fixtures, rub with a cloth soaked in kerosene. It removes scum and the smell will only linger for a short time.

To clean and polish stainless steel, simply moisten a cloth with undiluted white or cider vinegar and wipe clean. This method can also be used to remove heat stains on stainless steel cutlery.

Wash stainless steel cutlery by hand or in the dishwasher. Rinse off acid or salty foods immediately. Do not spill dry dishwasher detergent on wet cutlery as dark spots may result. Do not load stainless steel cutlery in the same basket section of dishwasher with silverware, as the silver may get damaged.

Do not let stainless steel pans boil dry, or overheat on the burner as it can cause discoloration. Stainless steel pans on burners do not distribute heat evenly and foods tend to stick in "hot spots", careful stirring of foods is important. Pans with a copper bottom, or "sandwich" layer of aluminium or copper hidden in the bottom overcome this problem.

Wash stainless steel utensils by hand or in dishwasher. If washed by hand, rinse well, and polish dry at once with soft towel to avoid spots and streaks. Dishwasher washing and drying does not leave these spots and streaks. If a bluish cast develops, it can be removed with silver polish.

*"The safest way to double your money is
to fold it over once and put it in your pocket."*

STAINLESS STEEL & CHROME

Acidic foods like salt, milk and milk products should be thoroughly washed off stainless steel utensils promptly or they can corrode the surface. Do not use harsh abrasives or steel wool on stainless steel.

Cooked-on food or grease can be removed from stainless steel utensils by using a fine abrasive cleaning powder or a paste of bicarbonate of soda and water. There are commercial stainless steel cleaners available.

In stainless steel sinks, use a perforated rubber or plastic mat to cut down on scratching and marking by pans and tableware. Wash with a solution of hand dish washing liquid detergent and water; or a solution of bicarbonate of soda and water. Rinse and polish dry with paper towel or soft cloth. Never use scouring powders or steel-wool as these will scratch the surface.

Brighten a sink by polishing with a cloth dipped in vinegar or ammonia, or dampen the sink and sprinkle a little bicarbonate of soda on a damp sponge and gently rub the surface, rinse well. Polish dry with paper towel.

To avoid chrome becoming scratched or loose its lustre, avoid using cleaning products with muriatic or sulfuric acids near chrome fixtures as even the fumes alone will slowly erode the surface. Check the labels of cleaning products to see if they include these acids.

Clean the chrome with soapy water or apple-cider vinegar mixed with water. When dry, cover the surface with a transparent protective coat, like furniture wax. This is very worthwhile to do in coastal areas, where the salt air can eat away at chrome surfaces.

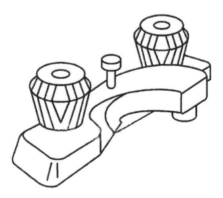

"Watch your thoughts, they become words.
Watch your words, they become actions.
Watch your actions, they become habits.
Watch your habits, they become character.
Watch your character, it becomes your destiny."

$\mathcal{C}$AR $\mathcal{M}$AINTENANCE

Take time to think - thoughts are the source of power.
Take time to play - play is the secret of perpetual youth. Take time to read -
reading is the fountain of wisdom.
Take time to pray - prayer can be a rock of strength
in time of trouble.
Take time to love - loving is what makes living worthwhile.
Take time to be friendly - friendships give life
a delicious flavour.
Take time to laugh - laughter is the music of the soul.
Take time to give - any day of the year is
too short for selfishness.
Take time to do your work well - pride in your work,
no matter what it is, nourishes the ego and the spirit.
Take time to show appreciation - thanks is the frosting
on the cake of life

REDUCE RUNNING COSTS OF CAR

Service a car regularly. A well- tuned and maintained vehicle will perform better and more economically.

Pumping the accelerator when the engine's cold wastes fuel. It's less wasteful to drive off immediately. Avoid doing higher speeds until the engine's warm. Drivers of automatic cars should move off as soon as the engine's running smoothly The accelerator pedal should only be given enough pressure to maintain a constant speed. This reduces tyre wear and mechanical repairs.

The battery should be kept at full charge. A regularly discharged battery will reduce the life of a battery.

Keep tyres at the recommended pressure. Under-inflated tyres can increase fuel consumption by 10% or more.

Keep the engine clean. It makes servicing easier and reduces the risk of grease and grime build-up hampering cables and other moving parts.

Fix small mechanical problem before it become more serious, saving on expensive repairs.

Run the car's air-conditioning at least for ten minutes each week, even in winter. This prevents the seals from drying out and the refrigerant from leaking. Using the air conditioner is a quick way to de-mist all windows on a winter morning.

Make sure to check the radiator level every fortnight and top it up if necessary. Use coolant, not water, as this will retard corrosion .

Make sure the fan belt is tensioned correctly (about 2cm free play only). A slipping belt can deteriorate quickly and cause wear to water pump and alternator bearings.

It pays to start winter with fresh engine oil. Change the oil as the old oil thickens and imposes extra strain on the engine, particularly on cold morning starts.

Avoid running a car on low fuel as this can shorten the life of the filter. It can get clogged with the debris building up in the petrol tank. Try to keep the tank at least a quarter full.

For every half tonne that a car weighs, it uses 700 litres of petrol a year. Keep the weight in the car light and save.

"Drive with care. Life has no spare."

CAR MAINTENANCE

Always read the safety warnings in the car owner's manual and any safety warning stickers under the hood.

When the engine has been running for any length of time, there are areas under the hood that can be very hot. Except for checking transmission fluid level, all checks should be done while the engine is turned off.

If the engine is running, avoid going near any belts or fans.

Never work on a car in a closed garage with the engine running. The carbon monoxide fumes from the exhaust can kill.

Do not wear loose clothing, ties or jewellery and keep long hair tied back when working over a running engine. Accidents can happen very quickly.

To remove corrosion from battery terminals, clean them with a mixture of baking soda and water. Disconnect the battery terminals before cleaning. Make a paste of 3 parts bicarbonate of soda to 1 part water, rub on to the affected area with a damp cloth. After cleaning and re-connecting the terminals, wipe them with petroleum jelly to prevent future corrosion. Be very careful when working around a battery as they contain a strong acid.

Use cola to clean the posts on a car battery.

Polish car chrome by applying full strength vinegar with a soft cloth.

Prevent rusting on chrome by polishing with methylated spirits, then rub on petroleum jelly for a lustrous shine. Or rub on plain flour, then polish with a soft cloth.

Coat chrome parts on a car with linseed oil to prevent them rusting. Clean the surface first, then rub on a light coat of linseed oil with a soft cloth.

To remove surface rust from chrome, crumple a piece of aluminium foil into a ball, dip it in water and rub on the rust area, rinse with clean water. This does not work on pitted rust areas.

Remove scratches on a car by rubbing the area with a wax crayon of a matching colour. Buff with a cloth.

"Nothing depreciates a car faster than a neighbour buying a new one."

CAR MAINTENANCE

Wash the car at least once a week. It stops grime causing permanent damage.

Sponge a car with 1pt(500ml) paraffin in a gallon of warm water. Wipe with a dry cloth.

Rub tar marks on car paint work with margarine, leave for a few hours, then wipe off with a damp cloth. Repeat, if necessary.

To remove tar from the car, mix bicarbonate of soda and enough water to make a paste, then rub on tar.

A few drops of lighter fluid or WD40 lubricating oil on a soft cloth will remove tar splatters from car paint-work. Wax the area afterwards.

To remove marks on cloth seats, first try to absorb as much as possible. Sponge or spray with dry-cleaning fluid. Apply warm water and vinegar. Rinse with water. Keep repeating until the stain is gone. Blot dry.

Ballpoint pen stains on car upholstery can be removed by mixing equal parts of fresh calcium and fuller's earth (available at most chemists), add a few drops of methylated spirits. Make into a thick paste, apply and wait until dry. Remove with damp cloth and dry thoroughly. Repeat procedure if stain persists.

Remove odours from car upholstery by sprinkling bicarbonate of soda directly on fabric car seats and carpets. Leave for 15 minutes then vacuum off.

Fill a small bowl with vinegar and place it on the floor of the car overnight to remove odours from the vehicle. The vinegar absorbs the smell.

For an effective car air freshener, place a fabric conditioner sheet (used in tumble dryers) underneath one of the front seats.

Wash car mats in the washing machine with a few old towels.

Put bicarbonate of soda in the car ashtray to reduce the smell and quickly extinguish cigarettes.

Clean car dashboards with baby wipes, they leave an anti-static layer, reducing dust.

"Energy is the 'Petrol' of life
Tact is the 'Lubricating Oil."

To keep car headlights free from mud, wipe them with a cut lemon once a week.

Use nylon netting to remove insects from windscreens and grills.

For stubborn insect marks, wet the windscreen and rub with full strength vinegar, or cola , or a wet sponge dipped in bicarbonate of soda.

On foggy mornings rub a cut, raw potato over the car windows. When it dries it will keep the windows clear.

Keep car windows frost free. Coat the windows the night before with a solution of three parts vinegar to one part water.

To keep a windscreen gleaming, wipe with a sponge dampened with cola or add 1tsp vinegar to the washer unit.

Clean windscreens with a cloth dipped in a bucket of warm water with a couple of tablespoons of white vinegar added. Polish with a clean, dry cloth. Smears can be removed with a cloth moistened with methylated spirits.

To hinder road film on windscreens, add 1tsp cream of tartar to the water when filling the windscreen washer unit. Or add 1tbsp ammonia per 1pt(600 ml) of water.

The plastic fittings in some new cars can give off fumes. These can cause a haze on the windows. Sponge with vinegar, rinse with water and wipe with a dry cloth.

Wiper blades should be changed every 6,000 to 10,000 miles.

Wiper blades will tend to streak when they are dirty. Take a paper towel with some window cleaner and clean the rubber blade whenever you clean the windshield.

Keep an old windscreen wiper in the car to remove any mist on side or rear windows. Or use a chalkboard eraser.

Rub a car aerial with wax paper every few months to keep them from corroding.

"Many a man who thinks he deserves a feather in his cap,
has a bee in his bonnet."

CAR MAINTENANCE

If you have trouble starting the car due to dampness on winter mornings, try using a hair dryer to dry out the engine.

To stop a radiator leak in an emergency, place a piece of chewing gum over the hole.

Alternatively cracking open an egg and putting into the boiling radiator will seal the hole on a short term basis. However be very careful opening a hot radiator.

For a hole in a radiator hose, wrap it with insulating tape or any available sticky tape for a temporary fix.

To remove oil stains on a garage floor, sprinkle the affected area with cat litter, and then rub the surface with a soft brick. Or you can first sprinkle dry sand over the stain to absorb as much oil as possible. Brush off, then wash with detergent. Or try washing with kerosene. Rinse with a mild solution of caustic soda, then rinse very thoroughly to remove all traces of the caustic solution.

Before requiring a car service or repair, check in the local area for a reputable garage. Ask friends and associates for recommendations or consult local consumer organisations.

When having the car serviced, note that the following have been checked:-
cooling system components, including pressure test;
battery and electrical system, including alternator output;
general engine performance;
fuel system;
all fluids;
ignition system;
tyres, including spare;
steering and suspension system, including shocks and struts
wheel balance and alignment, four wheel balance on front wheel drive vehicles;
braking system, including drums, rotors, hydraulics and electronic components;
emission control system components;
air conditioner/ heater /de-f roster;
instruments and gauges;
lights/ horn / mirrors;
windshield wipers and washers;
seat belts;
body evaluation / interior /exterior.

"Have you ever noticed?
Anybody going slower than you is an idiot,
and anyone going faster than you is a maniac."

TYRES

On front wheel drive cars, it is very important to rotate the tyres periodically because the front tyres wear faster than the rear.

Uneven tyre tread thickness, front to rear, will give uneven braking and poor handling, especially in the rain. Rotation extends the life of the tyre. Check the owner's manual for the proper rotation method.

Replace tyres in a matched set of four to keep the handling and braking traction of the car balanced.

When there is a humming noise from a tyre on a smooth road, check the rear tyres for a "saw-tooth" wear pattern by running your hand back and forth along the shoulder of the tyre tread. Be careful of debris or exposed steel belt wire. If it feels smooth in one direction, but jagged in the other, this may be the cause of the noise. This condition happens on some front wheel drive cars with tyres that have tread blocks on the shoulder of the tyre. Rotating this tyre to the other side of the car should even out this type of wear and quiet down the humming.

To assess tyres for inflation or alignment. At each tyre, take a coin and insert it in the tread at the inside, centre and outside:-
If the tread is deeper on the edges than in the centre, the tyre is over inflated.
If the tread is deeper in the centre than the edges, the tyre is under inflated.
If the tread is deeper on one side than the other, check the wheel alignment soon.
If the tyres have a "saw tooth" problem (as described above) the alignment should be checked as soon as possible as this can cause rapid tyre wear.

A wheel alignment consists of adjusting the angles of the wheels so that they are perpendicular to the ground and parallel to each other. The purpose of these adjustments is to maximise tyre life and a vehicle that tracks straight and true when driving along a straight and level road.

Another indication of out-of-alignment tyres is when the car continuously drifts or pulls to one side of the road when you let go of the wheel.

A car that is hard to keep in a straight line without constant steering corrections may need the tyres aligned.

"Some people have a one-track mind and very little traffic on it."

TYRES

After the wheel alignment is finished, the car should be driven on a straight and level road to check that the car goes straight and that the steering wheel is in the proper position with the spokes level. If you notice a problem, take the car back and have the technician drive it and fine-tune the alignment settings.

Out-of-balance tyres will cause a car to vibrate at certain speeds, usually between 50 and 70 mph. A tyre is out of balance when one section of the tyre is heavier than the others 1oz(25g) of imbalance on a front tyre is enough to cause a vibration in the steering wheel at about 60 mph.

To balance a wheel, the technician will mount it on a balancing machine that spins the wheel to locate the heavier part. He will then compensate for the heavy part by attaching a lead weight on the opposite side. It is noticeable how smooth a care drives after having all four wheels balanced.

Good quality tyres will hold their balance fairly well and only go out of balance very gradually. So if there is a noticeable vibration that wasn't there the previous day, it is possible that one of the lead balancing weights fell off. If the vibration is mostly in the steering wheel, the problem is most likely in a front wheel. If the vibration is mostly in the seat, the problem is in a rear wheel.

Invest in a good tyre gauge and keep it in the car. Improper tyre pressure can affect tyre wear as well as ride and handling. Always check tyres when they are cold. Use the manufacturers recommended tyre pressures. Tyre pressure tends to rise when driving due to heat build-up. Manufacturers have this in mind when they set the recommended cold pressures so do not let air out when the tyre gets hot. Check the tyre again when it cools off and the pressure should be back to normal. Tyre pressure will change with the seasons, so in winter months make sure they are not over inflated.

Over inflated tyres give less grip while under inflated tyres will weaken the casing and wear out the tread on the outside edges.

To remember the tyre pressure for a car, write the details on a piece of masking tape and stick it on the back of the tax disk holder.

*"To really know a man,
observe his behaviour with a woman,
a flat tyre and a child."*

Check for cuts and bulges on a regular basis. They are visual proof of internal damage and have the potential to become extremely dangerous.

If a blow out occurs, do not make sharp changes in direction, don't brake or use the clutch. Ease up on the accelerator and if the blow out is on a front wheel, use the handbrake (gently) to gradually slow the vehicle down.

To change a tyre, first make sure the vehicle is on firm level ground and away from traffic danger.

Turn off the engine, put on the hand brake and put into first gear.

Take the spare tyre, jack and tool kit from the boot of the car. Remove the hubcap using the flat end of the wrench., or with a screwdriver.

Loosen the nuts on the wheel by turning them left or anti-clockwise.

If you do not know where the jacking point is on the car, check the owner's manual. There is generally a reinforced spot on the frame.

Place the jack under this area and making sure the jack is level, start jacking slowly. Only raise the car enough to allow the wheel to come of easily.

Remove the wheel nuts and put them somewhere safe. Remove the wheel and set aside.

Place the spare wheel on the car and tighten the nuts. Let the car down slowly. Tighten one nut then skip one and tighten the next, continuing until all the nuts are tight.

Replace the hubcap and put all tools and spare wheel into the boot.

Narrow spare tires should only be used for a short distance and at a speed not over 50mph.

If all four wheel nuts get lost from one wheel of a car, take one nut off the other three wheels to get you to the garage

Tires deflate as temperature decreases - one pound of pressure for every 10 degrees of temperature drop.

"The straight and narrow path is the only one
which does not seem to have a traffic problem."

Sensible Motoring

Before setting off on a journey, check the petrol and oil levels, inflation of tyres and that no warning lights are showing on the dash.

Adjust the seat so that the steering wheels and foot pedals are within easy reach. When you straighten your left leg you should be able to push the clutch down without any effort.

The seat belt should feel comfortable and not cut into the shoulder. When fastened it should lie over the middle of the shoulder, down across the middle of the chest and over the hipbone.

Keep your arms at a comfortable distance apart on the steering wheel. They should be slightly bent with the hands in a ten-to-two or a quarter-to -three position on the wheel.

The shoulders should be relaxed with the head held upright and chin tucked in to avoid neck strain.

Position the rear view mirror so that you must sit upright to use it.

Use the mirrors often and be constantly aware of the traffic around you.

The seat should lean back slightly for a well-balanced position.

When getting out of the car, turn the whole body towards the open door, place the feet on the ground, then stand up.

On long journeys stop regularly (in a safe parking area) and stretch. Concentrate, stay alert and never drive when tired or after consuming alcohol.

Be careful when taking medicine as some over the counter, cold remedies or travel sickness medication can cause drowsiness.

Do not use a mobile phone when driving

Children or babies travelling in a car must be secured in safe car seats.

Be courteous on the road - give way to pedestrians, allow vehicles to come out of side roads when safe to do so. Do not have an aggressive or competitive attitude.

"All's fair in love, war and car parking!"

When parking do not obstruct driveways or other vehicles. Be especially carefully when parking near schools.

Avoid changing gear or braking when turning a corner as this can affect the car's stability. Speed and gear change should be modified as you approach a bend.

Drive at a safe distance from the car in front of you. In good weather and visibility give a two-second gap - as the car in front passes a stationary object (eg a lamp-post) say "only a fool breaks the two second rule". If you pass the object before you have said this then you are driving too close.

In wet weather a four second gap is required and in fog or snow even longer.

When planning to overtake a vehicle, do not drive up too close to it, as this will obscure the view of the road ahead.

In heavy rain use dipped headlights. Do not use fog lights unnecessarily as they can dazzle the driver behind you.

Make sure that the car headlights are clean.

When driving through a flooded part of a road where the water comes up to the bottom of the wheel hubs, approach slowly with fairly high revs in a low gear. Avoid stalling the engine as water can get sucked into the exhaust pipe. Once out of the flood apply the brakes hard several times to dry them out.

If you get stuck in snow or on ice, do not spin the wheels as this will melt the frozen surface making the problem worse.

Place gravel, an old sack, car mat or twigs, etc. under the front of the driving wheels, select second gear and let the clutch in slowly with minimum acceleration.

Carry an emergency kit - first aid kit, hazard warning triangle, torch and towrope. A well-maintained spare wheel, tyre changing tools and a jack must always be in a vehicle.

Good Motoring!

*"We know what happens to people
who stay in the middle of the road - they get run over."*

MEASUREMENTS

Length

ins	mm	mm	ins
1/64	0.397	1	0.039
1/32	0.794	2	0.079
1/16	0.587	3	0.118
1/8	3.175	4	0.158
1/4	6.350	5	0.197
1/2	12.700	6	0.236
3/4	19.050	7	0.276
1	25.400	8	0.315
12(1ft)	304.800	9	0.354
36(1yd)	914.400	10(1cm)	0.394
		1000(1m)	39.370

Area

1sq in	6.452sq cm	1sq cm	0.155sq.in
1sq ft	929.030sq cm	1sq m	1.196sq yd
1sq yd	0.836sq m		

Weight

1oz	28.350g	1g	0.352oz
1lb	0.454kg	1kg	2.205lb
1cwt	50.802kg	1metric ton	0.984tons
1ton	1.016metric tons		

Capacity

1fl oz	2.841cl	1cl	0.352fl oz
1pt	0.568ltr	1ltr	1.760pt
1gall	4.546ltr		

Volume

1cu in	16.387cu.cm	1cu cm	0.061cu in
1cu ft	0.028cu m	1cu m	1.308cu yd
1cu yd	0.765cu m		

Conversion

Inches to centimetres	x	2.540
Yards to metres	x	0.914
Miles to kilometres	x	1.609
Pints to litres	x	0.578
Gallons to litres	x	4.546
Ounces to grams	x	28.350
Pounds to kilograms	x	0.454

When measuring or weighing use either imperial or metric

GLOSSARY

OF
DIY TERMS

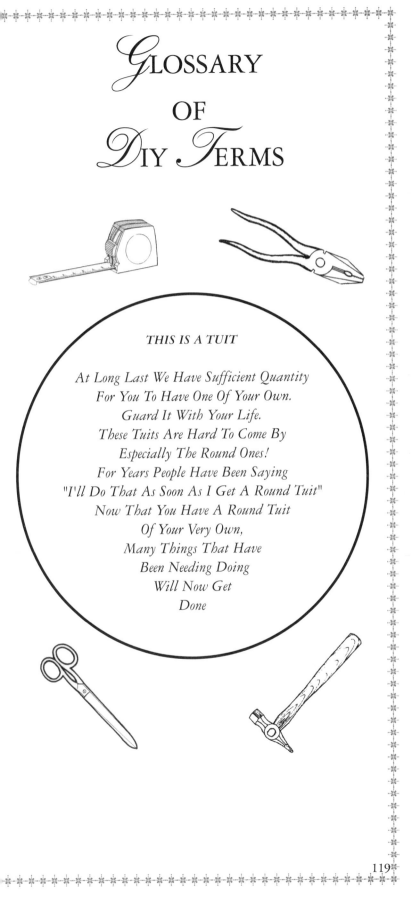

THIS IS A TUIT

At Long Last We Have Sufficient Quantity
For You To Have One Of Your Own.
Guard It With Your Life.
These Tuits Are Hard To Come By
Especially The Round Ones!
For Years People Have Been Saying
"I'll Do That As Soon As I Get A Round Tuit"
Now That You Have A Round Tuit
Of Your Very Own,
Many Things That Have
Been Needing Doing
Will Now Get
Done

AMPERE: the rate of flow of electricity through electric wires.

AIR DUCT : pipes carrying warm air and cold air to rooms and back to furnace or air conditioning system.

BACKFILL : the gravel or earth replaced in the space around a building wall after foundations are in place.

BALUSTRADE: a row of balusters topped by a rail, edging a balcony or a staircase.

BATTEN : small narrow strips covering joints between wider boards on exterior building surfaces.

BEAM: one of the principal horizontal wood or steel members of a building.

BEARING WALL: a wall supporting a floor or roof of a building.

BLEEDING: seeping of gum or resin from lumber. Term is also used in referring to the process of drawing air from water pipes.

BRACE: a piece of wood or other material used to form a triangle and stiffen some part of a structure.

BUTT JOINT: joining point of two pieces of wood.

CASEMENT: a window sash opening on hinges at the vertical edge.

CASING: door and window framing.

CAVITY WALL: a hollow wall formed by firmly linked masonry walls, providing an insulating air space between.

CHASE: a groove in a masonry wall or through a floor to accommodate pipes or ducts.

CHIMNEY CAP: concrete capping around the top of chimney bricks to protect the masonry from the elements.

CIRCUIT BREAKER: a safety device to open or break an electric circuit automatically when it becomes overloaded.

COPING TILE: used to cap or cover the top of a masonry wall.

CORNER BEAD: a strip of wood or metal for protecting the external corners of plastered walls.

DORMER: the projecting frame of a recess in a sloping roof.

DOWNSPOUT: a spout carrying rain water from a roof or gutters.

DRY WALL: a wall surface of plasterboard or material other than plaster.

EAVES: the extension of roof beyond house walls.

EFFLORESCENCE: white powder that forms on the surface of brick.

FASCIA: a flat horizontal member of a cornice placed in a vertical position.

FLASHING: non-corrosive metal used around angles or junctions in roofs and exterior walls to prevent leaks, generally lead is used.

FLOOR JOISTS: framing pieces that rest on walls and interior beams or girders.

FLUE: a passageway in a chimney to allow smoke, gases or fumes to escape to the outside air.

FOOTING: concrete base on which a foundation sits.

FOUNDATION: walls of masonry or concrete below ground level on which the structure of a building is built.

FUSE: a short plug in an electric panel box that opens and breaks an electrical circuit when it becomes overloaded.

GABLE: the triangular part of a wall under the inverted "v" of the roof-line.

GIRDER: A main member supporting the joists that carry the flooring boards and the weight of a floor or partition.

GLAZING: fitting glass into windows or doors.

GREEN LUMBER: lumber prior to drying

GUTTER: a channel at the eaves for draining away rain-water.

HARDWOOD: the close-grained wood from broad-leaved trees such as oak or maple.

HIP ROOF: a roof slanting upwards on three or four sides.

HIP: the external angle formed by the juncture of two slopes of a roof.

JOIST: a small rectangular sectional member arranged parallel from wall to wall in a building, or resting on beams or girders.

KILN-DRIED; artificial drying of lumber, superior to most lumber that is air-dried.

LATHS: thin narrow strips of wood nailed to rafters, ceiling joists, wall studs, etc as a base for slates, tiles, or plastering.

LINTEL: the top piece over a door or window supporting the walls above the opening.

LOAD-BEARING WALL: a strong wall capable of supporting weight.

MASONRY: walls built by a mason, using brick, stone, tile or similar materials.

MOULDING: a prepared strip of decorative material with a plain or curved narrow surface used for ornamental application. Often these strips are used to hide gaps at wall junctures.

NEWEL: the upright post or the upright formed by the inner or smaller ends of steps about which steps of a circular staircase wind. In a straight flight staircase, the main post at the foot or the secondary post at a landing.

PITCH: the angle of slope of a roof.

PLASTERBOARD: gypsum board, used instead of plaster.

POINTING: the filling of joints in masonry with mortar to improve appearance or protect against weather.

RADIANT HEAT: produced by electric coils, hot water or steam pipes embedded in floors, ceilings, or walls to heat rooms.

RAFTER: One of a series of structural roof members spanning from an exterior wall to a centre ridge beam.

REINFORCED CONCRETE: concrete strengthened with wire or metal bars.

RIDGE POLE: a thick longitudinal plank to which the ridge rafters of a roof are attached.

RISER: the upright piece of a stair step, from tread to tread.

SASH: the movable part of a window frame in which panes of glass are set in a window or door.

SEEPAGE PIT: a sewage disposal system composed of a septic tank and a connected cesspool.

SEPTIC TANK: a sewage settling tank in which part of the sewage is converted into gas and sludge before the remaining waste is discharged by gravity into a leaching bed underground.

SKIRTINGS: narrow boards around the bottom of a wall.

SOFFIT: the visible underside of beams or eaves.

SOFTWOOD: wood from a cone-bearing tree.

SUB-FLOOR: in timber floors it is usually plywood sheets nailed directly to the floor joists to receive the finished flooring. In concrete floors the sub-floor refers to the structural floor prior to screeding.

TOENAIL: driving nails at an angle into corners or other joints.

TONGUE-AND-GROOVE: carpentry joint in which the jutting edge of one board fits into the grooved end of a similar board.

TRAP: A bend in a water pipe to hold water so gases will not escape from the plumbing system into the house.

TREAD: the horizontal part of a stair step.

TRUSS: a combination of structural members usually arranged in triangular units to form a rigid framework for spanning between load-bearing walls.

VENT PIPE: a pipe allowing gas to escape from plumbing systems.

VOLTAGE: the force of flow of electricity through wires and cables from the mains supply.

VENETIAN WINDOW: a window with one large fixed central pane and smaller panes at each side.

WATTS: the measurement of the amount of electricity used at any moment by equipment. It is calculated by multiplying the amperage by the voltage.

NDEX

abrasive, 14, 15, 70, 97, 117
acetone, 25
adhesive, 32, 33, 35, 36, 39,
81, 82, 84, 97, 98, 109, 110,
113
aggregate, 112
air filters, 73
aluminium, 24, 36, 49, 71,
79, 82, 98, 116, 121
aluminium, 18, 90, 91

bath, 20, 37, 38, 43, 44, 48,
85
battery, 54, 62, 119, 120, 124
bench grinders, 58
blowtorch, 17, 18, 45, 46
boiler, 37-40
bolts, 69, 80, 92
brick, 18, 69, 75, 113, 114,
123, 132-134
brushes, 13, 16, 23-26
bucket, 15-17, 26, 29, 34, 40,
45, 48, 49, 58, 93, 122
bulbs, 53, 55

car, 58, 93, 102, 119-129
carpentry, 60, 75, 136
cast iron, 114, 115
caulk, 12, 13, 52, 85, 86, 87
caustic soda, 16, 17, 41, 123
ceiling, 11, 20, 24, 28, 29, 32,
33, 51, 72, 134, 135
cellulose filler, 12
cement, 18, 23, 27, 59, 77,
81, 102, 111-113
chair, 95
chalk-line, 59
chemicals, 16, 23
chipboard, 77, 105
chisel, 60, 62, 63, 65, 69, 70,
83, 98, 110, 113
chrome, 77, 117, 120, 121
chuck key, 72, 90

circular saw, 66, 67, 90
cistern, 41, 42
clamping, 68, 70, 83
clamps, 15, 68, 83, 84
concrete, 63, 78, 85, 111-113,
132-135
condensation, 19, 39, 42
coping saw, 65
copper pipe, 39, 49
craft knife, 60
cupboard, 95, 105

decorating, 10, 11
door, 10, 24, 26, 27, 32, 35,
44, 52, 69, 85, 96-99, 128,
132-135
downspout, 102
drain-pipes, 18
drill, 15, 65, 66, 71-73, 76,
84, 90, 107, 109, 110

electrical appliances, 32, 51,
53, 54, 62, 85, 111
electric drill, 18, 53
electricity, 46, 51, 53-55, 90,
91, 132, 136
electronic equipment, 54
emery paper/cloth, 13, 14
emulsion, 11, 18-20, 29, 31
energy-saving, 55
epoxy, 39, 82
extension cables, 51
exterior paint, 31

files, 69, 70, 71
fire extinguisher, 54, 88
first aid kit, 88, 129
flex, 53
float ball, 41
floorboards, 69, 76, 104, 107

INDEX

flooring, 68, 104-106, 134, 135
flux, 45-48
foam pads, 24
fret saw, 65
frozen pipe, 40
fungicidal liquid, 32
furniture, 10, 12, 13, 83, 84, 96, 103, 105, 114, 117
fuse, 51-53, 55, 56

glass, 13, 17, 29, 45, 59, 65, 73, 80, 81, 98-100, 109, 134, 135
glue, 33-35, 41, 63, 77, 79-85, 95, 107
goggles, 16, 32, 58, 65, 68, 72, 75, 76, 88, 89, 98, 109
grout, 109-111
gutters, 30, 101, 133

hacksaw, 14, 65-67, 79
hammer, 21, 40, 63-65, 72, 75-77, 89, 98, 100, 107, 110
hardboard, 18, 34, 96, 98, 105
hot air gun, 17
hot water tank, 38
immersion heaters, 52, 55
insect marks, 122

knotting, 18

ladder, 89, 90-93, 101
laminate, 83, 106
leaks, 39, 85, 133
levels, 59
light fixtures, 12
lining paper, 34

linseed oil, 63, 91, 95, 98-100, 121
lock, 69, 70, 79, 97, 98

magnet, 48, 58, 61, 62, 73
mallet, 63
manual, 90
marble, 108, 109
masking tape, 13, 14, 21, 22, 26, 27, 30, 61, 68, 69, 71, 72, 83, 99, 108, 109, 110, 126
masonry, 13, 31, 65, 72, 75, 110, 112, 132, 133, 135
measurements, 10, 33, 58, 60, 61, 78, 99, 106, 130
metal, 10, 13, 16-19, 23, 26, 30, 45, 46, 49, 58, 59, 61, 63, 65, 66, 71-73, 77-82, 84, 89, 90, 99, 100, 102, 107, 109, 113, 115, 133, 135
mineral spirits, 25
mirrors, 73, 77, 124, 128
mitre saw, 65
monkey wrench, 69
mortar, 69, 82, 109, 111, 112, 135

nails, 11, 32, 34, 53, 63-65, 69, 73, 75-77, 80-82, 84, 90, 92, 135

oil paint, 11, 25, 36
oilstone, 57

paint, 10-14, 16-36, 49, 61, 79, 80, 81, 83, 84, 86, 87, 91, 93, 95, 96, 102, 114, 121
paint scrapers, 13

INDEX

paint smell, 19, 29, 43, 53, 116, 122
paint strippers, 18
paintbrushes, 22, 25
painting, 11, 13, 16, 19, 20, 22-24, 26-32, 87, 101, 105
panel pin, 75
paraffin, 13, 14, 25, 43, 49, 67, 71, 76, 98, 121
pencil, 34, 58, 60, 95, 97, 106
petroleum jelly, 39, 41, 78, 81, 87, 120
pipe, 19, 22, 23, 29, 30, 37-42, 47-49, 53, 54, 62, 64-69, 92, 97, 101, 129, 132, 135, 136
plane, 69, 70
plaster, 11-14, 17, 18, 32, 36, 76, 82, 113, 133, 135
plastic sheeting, 12
pliers, 38, 68, 69, 77, 80, 99
plug, 41, 48, 51-54, 73, 80, 89, 133
plugs, 51, 53, 62, 110
plumb bob/line, 35, 59, 109
plywood, 68, 96, 105, 106, 112, 135
power sanders, 15
primer, 18, 19, 31, 32, 98
putty, 12, 16, 71, 73, 80, 86, 95, 98-102
putty knife, 12, 13, 16, 86, 98, 100, 102

radiator, 10, 19, 23, 29, 30, 40, 49, 119, 123
rasp, 71
roller, 20, 22, 24, 25, 28, 29, 35
ruler, 34, 35, 60, 61, 99
rust, 13, 14, 19, 30, 46, 49, 68, 75, 88, 109, 114-116, 121

safety, 87
sanding,, 14, 89
sandpaper, 12-15, 18, 49, 64, 97
satellite dish, 55
saw, 65-68, 83, 106, 109, 124, 125
sawdust, 82
scissors,, 34
scraper, 17, 32, 83
screw, 34, 40, 41, 49, 52-54, 58, 62, 73, 75-80, 82, 84, 86, 90, 91, 93, 96, 107, 110
screwdriver, 51, 52, 61, 62, 69, 77, 97, 127
sealant, 44, 85-87, 102
shower, 43, 44, 85
silicone, 13, 52, 85-87, 102
sink, 11, 41, 42, 48, 117
sizing, 35
skirtings, 29
slate, 114
soldering, 45-48, 98
solvent, 16, 24, 25, 84, 108
spanners, 69
spray gun, 28
spur, 56
square, 58
stainless steel, 76, 78, 115-117
stairs, 26, 27, 92, 107
steel wool, 13-16, 47, 49, 79, 82, 84, 100, 115, 117
step ladder, 13, 91
stone, 58, 112, 114, 134
stop-valve, 38
stripping paint, 15, 17
stripping paper, 33
sugar soap, 11

tap, 21, 37, 40, 48, 64, 98
tape measure, 58, 59
tile, 10, 20, 44, 65, 69, 73, 85, 109-111, 134

INDEX

timber, 17, 18, 65-67, 75, 78, 84, 98, 104, 106
toilet, 37, 38, 41, 42
toolbox, 58, 71
tools, 13, 26, 34, 51, 53, 57-61, 63, 64, 70, 73, 88-90, 93, 113, 127, 129
turpentine, 43, 61, 73, 95, 99
tyres, 119, 124-127

undercoat, 18, 19, 30
upholstery, 10, 75, 121

varnish, 16
veneer, 68, 83, 104
vinegar, 17, 25, 29, 30, 33, 41-45, 73, 79, 80, 84, 95, 96, 113, 116, 117, 120-123

wallpaper, 10, 11, 18, 28, 32-36, 107
wallpaper paste, 18, 32
walls, 11, 13, 17, 19, 20, 24, 28, 31-35, 51, 63, 75, 78, 85, 97, 111, 132-136
washing soda,, 41
water meter, 38
wheel, 15, 124-129
white spirits, 20
window, 10, 12, 17, 19, 27, 29, 45, 85, 93, 95, 98, 100, 123, 132-136
window-frames, 17
windows, 24, 32, 35, 108, 119, 122, 123, 134
windscreens, 122
wiper blades, 123
wire brush, 13
wires, 46, 48, 51-55, 132, 136

wood, 10, 13-15, 17-20, 25, 32, 41, 63-72, 75-84, 90-98, 101, 104-107, 110, 113-132-135
workshop, 51, 76, 88, 89